EXCAVATION

EXCAVATION

JEAN GOULBOURNE

PEEPAL TREE

First published in Great Britain in 1997
Peepal Tree Press Ltd
17 King's Avenue
Leeds LS6 1QS
England

ISBN 1-900715-12-0

CHAPTER 1

The minibus moved northwards into the dark. The shadows of the evening had already been gathering when they boarded, and now those in the minibus sat silent in their seats. They were mostly strangers, and not being able to see each other's faces discouraged talk. There was time enough for that. They would be living together for the next four weeks.

Carla pressed her face against the window, staring into the darkness outside. The only thing she could hear was the sound of the wheels moving against the asphalt road. Trees and houses sped by. The lights punctuating the darkness made Carla think of the peenie wallies and nights at home in the south of the island, close to the coast. There she had often gone outside to watch the stars, when there was no cloud and they seemed like brilliant pinpricks against the dark sky. Her father had pointed out the different constellations and told her that the earth on which she stood was part of it all.

"Are peenie wallies stars too, Daddy?" she had asked. He had smiled and taken her hands.

"No, Carla," he had said, "they're tiny insects. The stars are huge heavenly bodies, but far away. So very, very far away they seem small."

A jolt as the minibus hit a pothole brought her back to the present and she turned to look at the other travellers. They seemed either to be sleeping or lost in their own thoughts. She could just see the white faces of the two young Americans and the Professor's greying hair stood out against the blackness of his face. She wondered what it was going to be like to work so closely with him. He had come to the university just last year, the second year of her course, with the reputation of being a brilliant and controversial scholar. A genuine revolutionary, unlike so many of the other lecturers who pretended to be radicals but soon settled down to the life of the comfortable middle class, forgetting all those whose cause they had pretended to support.

Carla glanced briefly at David, one of the two Americans. He was handsome and on the evidence of their brief meeting before they boarded the bus, seemed an outgoing, happy-go-lucky kind of boy. She wondered why he had chosen to come to Jamaica for this part of his research. Perhaps he saw it as the place to frolic as a tourist rather than as a place to work, especially here on the north coast. Maybe he wanted to do both. She would see.

The other white boy, Martin, seemed even younger, immature and unsure of himself. He stared out of the window at the night outside, ignoring the others. Reserved and remote, Carla decided. She glanced back at David again.

He was thinking how cold his native Chicago had been when he had left, though it would soon be spring. Spring was special to him for he felt that it always brought some new growth in himself. Yet he loved what he had so far seen of Jamaica: the greener than green of the trees, the dark-blue sea flecked with green, and moving, always moving like a restless, untamed child. There was something in this wildness that appealed to him, but he also felt that what this country needed was taming: the grass, the hedges, the trees and the forests – and the people.

He had seen laughter in the eyes of the children, had felt desire stir as he watched the swaying bodies of the women. Tall, fat, large, small or thin: he had felt his sexual urges awakening and had wondered at it. He had never desired a black woman before. At home they were the dark, forbidden fruit he had never wished to pluck. It was being abroad that did it. In the distance he saw the flash of the wings of a white bird. Perhaps an owl.

He looked at the young girl sitting to the right of him. Her name was Carla, he remembered. She was really pretty. Four weeks gave him the chance to get to know her better; the possibilities excited him. She seemed shy and uncertain; perhaps she'd be glad of someone to bring her out of herself. How long would it take to get close to her? Maybe if he went swimming with her that would be a start. The hotel was close to the beach and to Ocho Rios, one of the chief tourist spots in the island. Dancing maybe? He would see.

He glanced at the Professor. He was so much blacker than Carla. In his neighbourhood there were only a handful of middle-class black people, and he'd never had a close friend from among their children. At University the black students mostly kept to themselves. There were some he got on well with, but they too went their separate ways at the end of classes. He had never been to a black person's home. He had read about the Civil Rights movement, busing and the racial conflicts of the nineteen sixties. He knew his mother hated blacks, as did many of his relatives. His father was a bit more liberal, but heaven forbid he should take a black girl home, even just as a friend. He knew that though much had been achieved, Black Americans still had to struggle for social equality.

He didn't like the racist talk of some of the people he knew and had sometimes quietly objected. As an archaeology student, he'd always had white tutors, white professors, white fellow students. He'd been ashamed when he and Martin had been met at the airport by an impeccably dressed man in a navy-blue bush jacket suit and he'd taken him for a chauffeur sent to pick them up. The 'chauffeur' had shaken hands with them and introduced himself as the Professor of Archaeology at the island's university.

"Christ!" Martin had exclaimed when they were alone in their room. "A black Professor of Archaeology? These people have made progress. I've never been taught by a black Prof before. Black high school teachers yes, but a black Prof of Archaeology? Hardly."

"The world's changing fast," David said.

Martin had grinned, "Well, let's see him perform and then we can judge. As long as he's got there by merit, I've no problems with that. What I object to back home is this positive discrimination thing, all these quotas. That's not equal rights. But you have to wonder about their capacity to run things when you look at what's happening in Africa, not to mention here."

"Look at South Africa," David had said. " Doesn't Mandela give you hope?"

"Maybe," Martin had replied. "Seems like a good guy, but running the whole country – and after him?"

David thought about this conversation as the van moved on in the dark. Black people had made tremendous strides. It was not just in sports and music that Black Americans were excelling. He knew little about contemporary Jamaica except that it was where Bob Marley came from, and his music had certainly appealed to him. He wondered about Martin. He was a businessman's son from down in the South. He didn't think he was a racist. If he was, why had he come on this study visit? He glanced at Professor Milton. How would he and

Martin be treated, as the only whites on this field trip? He looked again at the girl who sat close to the window. Her hair was straightened. Chemically done. Though maybe this girl had Indian blood in her. Or was it white? From his reading of Caribbean history he knew that the white managers and overseers on the plantations had never been satisfied with their wives. They had succumbed to their desires for black slave-women and the children they had fathered had in turn been made to work on the plantation. He smiled in her direction, but she was still looking outside.

The minibus lurched. It had either slipped into a pothole or run over an animal. Maybe a mongoose or a rat. Outside coconut trees stood tall and stark against the sky. Against the horizon, they looked blue-black, elegant even. The shrubbery had changed somewhat as they entered each stage of the journey. They had left the lush green hills and entered beach country with its wild grape trees and coconut trees. In some areas the coconut trees stood bare, stark reminders of the diseases that had destroyed so many in the past.

Carla glanced again at the white boy beside her. He had been staring at her. She flushed, confused. She disliked being stared at, even though she should have been used to it by now. At twenty-two she'd had her share of admirers, had fallen in and out of something like love a couple times, but it had never been the real thing. She looked out at the dark. The moon had just come up. Sickle-shaped, it held water. Her father had told her that when the moon looked as though it carried a heavy load of water there was going to be rain. She thought of her family again and felt homesick. She glanced around. The Professor was looking at her.

"It's quite cool tonight," he said quietly.

Carla smiled, but it was the driver who replied, "Yes sah. Though is March. Times cold this year."

The Professor hugged his arms together and looked at Carla again. She always seemed so pensive. He wondered why she got under his skin so much. He'd had his flings but no woman, not even his wife, had affected him as much as this girl. She rarely spoke in class, seemed to like her own company, yet she gave him the best essays he had read in a long time. They were... provocative. Yes, that was the word, provocative. As provocative as her little nose and the hair that would have been curly if she had not made it straighter with those chemicals. Why was the girl so silent?

The Professor thought of the years away from Jamaica. This was his first archaeological dig in his own country. He had taught at universities abroad and had led digs with his students and other teachers to minor archaeological sites in Europe and Asia. Now that he was getting older, he had felt the need for home. When the university had begun offering archaeology as a course for its history students, he had been glad to accept the offer to come and head the unit.

There was the smell of decaying vegetation in the air, the pungent smell of animal manure and cultivation. The Professor peered through the window. The darkness was now relieved only by the moon. He glanced at his watch. Eight o' clock. Time for a meal. He wondered what the hotel would have waiting for them when they arrived, and whether it would be good.

He'd taken a good look at the place before deciding to spend the university's money there. Although it was small and slightly ramshackle, he had liked it. He liked the atmosphere and the price. It was close to the site and the sea, and not too near the bustle of Ocho Rios with its noisy night life. They were not likely to be disturbed there. It was the sort of place that attracted him.

As he thought about the coming meal he looked across to the African who had come to assist him in leading the excavation. Kwame had trained initially in Ghana but had finished his studies in the USA. He had come to join him in the department and though he was much younger and less experienced, he had nevertheless proved to be of great value. Many of the slaves who had lived on the plantation they were going to excavate had come from the area around Ghana, from the Ashanti tribe. An aggressive people, they had been greatly feared. Kwame, though, seemed as soft as a dove.

Kwame saw the Professor looking towards him and nodded in return. He felt the excitement of the night move in his veins. He had been on many digs before, but this was his first in the Caribbean. He had joined the history department only recently, his appointment due no doubt to Professor Milton's support. He had published some well-received papers dealing with excavations in Kumase in Ghana but also with the cultural backgrounds of the slaves who had been brought to the Caribbean from his area. He knew that Professor Milton had pressed for the appointment of an African scholar who would bring that expertise to the study of African survivals in the Caribbean. His time in America had left him feeling how American most African Americans were. Here in Jamaica, he sensed that Africa was never far below the surface of things.

This field trip was the culmination of what had long absorbed his interest. Even as a child, when he learnt that many of his people had been taken to the Caribbean and the Americas as slaves, he had been curious as well as angry about what had happened to them. For most Ghanaians the slave trade was simply something that had happened in the past, another colonial crime studied in a few lessons at school and then something to be forgotten.

For him, the story of his people's forced departure would not go away. As a child, thinking about it had made him angry – with the Europeans who had stolen away his people, and with those Africans who had sold their fellows into slavery. But as he got older he had begun to see such anger was futile, though his sense of grief for what Africans had suffered in the middle passage remained. Later his feelings had grown into a curiosity about what had happened to those who had made the crossing. He had read widely but had long wanted to see for himself, to compare the life of his own tribe with the lives of Africans in the new world. How had his people withstood the pressures of another world? They were a people tied to tradition and worship of their ancestors. How had they survived the regimented brutalities of plantation labour, a form of agriculture so alien to their traditions of subsistence farming and reverence for the land. How had they assimilated a new culture, a new language, a new life? He hoped the excavation would bring him closer to that past.

He looked outside at the lights from the houses that stood a little back from the road. They were strong concrete houses, built to withstand any hurricane. And as the minibus moved closer to Ocho Rios, or Ochie as many Jamaicans called it, the houses became larger and more imposing.

This world was new and strange, yet familiar. It was thousands of miles away from Ghana but was home to thousands of his own people. He looked at Akete, a Rastafarian, a mature student. He had read about the Rastafarians and their spiritual journey back to Africa. Akete seemed very serious. It would be good to get to know him better.

Akete was debating whether he could smoke a spliff in the minibus. Would the professor mind? He really needed to have a draw. It seemed as though fresh air always made him want to smoke. He took the spliff from his pocket, lit it and took a pull.

"Akete," said the Professor as he smelt the weed, "be careful. That thing will blow your mind."

Akete grinned. "I man used to it, Prof," he said. This was his first excavation and it meant a lot to him. This trip back into the past would contribute to the mission Jah had sent him on, to help to liberate black people from their mental chains. He had named himself Akete, when he first came to appreciate his blackness and the richness of his heritage. He felt that it fitted him, and he loved the look in the eyes of strangers when he introduced himself. 'Akete', like a warrior of old. He had grown up in a strongly middle-class family but had left it for the ghetto life whilst still a youth. That was where he belonged now, and he would use his skills to teach and uplift his people. His middle-class parents, like many people with 'ambition', still looked to the white man for direction. He, Akete, was a black man with a past, who had read deeply into African history. His future was that of a strong, liberated African man.

But he knew that no matter how well the streets could teach him, he also needed to know his books. So he and his woman had got together to see him through university. At thirty-one, he had a woman, Shadi, and a child, Sheba. He lived in rented rooms close to Trench Town. He had known and worshipped Bob Marley, whom he saw as another Garvey come to spread the word of black man's liberation.

Akete smoked, thinking of the days ahead of him. Four weeks. The white men in the minibus would learn more of the black man's past. He wondered why they had chosen this island rather than one of their own little places in Europe, the Greek islands perhaps. But he would certainly let them know more of the black man's history. Their race had tried to destroy his people's culture, and would have succeeded but for the resilience of his race.

Akete looked at the other occupants of the van, at the Professor whom he admired immensely, at Kwame who, as an African, he wanted to know better, and also at the three girls. Monica and Sonia he thought he understood, but Carla was a mystery. She was pretty, yet so shy and retiring and innocent. Akete blew the smoke upwards in the van. She reminded him of Shadi before they had come together. Shadi had been a country girl, a domestic helper who had known so little about life in the city. In a lot of ways she had remained innocent. He caught one of the white boys looking at Carla. She looked so vulnerable. He would protect this daughter.

The minibus sped on, bumping into potholes now and again.

"The man driving too fast," Akete observed aloud as he sent a curl of smoke over his head.

"Mi wan' reach back home tonight," the driver said in defence.

He slipped into fourth gear and the wheels flew over the asphalt.

"I man want to go back home safe to my baby mother too, so I beg you cool it," countered Akete.

In the darkness he felt rather than saw the driver smile. He slipped back into second gear. The smell of the sea outside permeated everything. The van slowed as they approached the turning. The passengers relaxed a little.

The other two occupants of the minibus, Sonia and Monica, were twins. Unusually, they had been quiet during the journey, but that was only because they were tired. They were popular, outgoing, athletic girls whose attractiveness lay in their ability to socialise and their readiness to listen. Their room on campus was a haven for the sick and the sick at heart. Headache or heartache, they went to the twins who took them in and ministered to them. Now Sonia sat slumped with her eyes closed. Monica was barely awake. It had been a long hard day.

Outside the night hung like a pall. Through the open window the smell of salt grew stronger. They were approaching their destination.

The road into the hotel compound was even more bumpy than the highway. The sound of the waves moving restlessly to and fro, and the lighter sound of crickets chirping gave the whole place the feel of deep countryside. Once again the Professor was happy that he had found a place like this, away from the prying eyes of tourists, pimps and prostitutes.

The trees grew close to the driveway, whose potholes were full of water. Here and there cultivated shrubs grew as though the owner was trying in vain to domesticate the place.

A small two-storey building came into view, with outbuildings scattered haphazardly about the grounds. The main building was square with white walls and welcoming lights in its French windows. A veranda ran from the front all the way round to the back of the building, wooden chairs placed along its walls. Enclosing the veranda was white-painted fretwork, but chipped and badly in need of repainting and repair. But it looked homely, a welcome anachronism so near to the expensive and anonymous-looking hotels along the north coast. It reminded the Professor of his dead grandparents' house way back in his childhood in Portland. It had looked like this, with the same air about it. He had often wondered if houses had their own personalities, living their own lives as it were.

A dog bounded up to them and barked sharply, but retreated when a tall, slim, figure came out to meet them. It was their host, the man who owned and ran the tiny hotel with the help of his unmarried daughter and a few helpers.

"Come on in! Come on in! We're ready for you," he said.

David looked around. He liked this place. It was different from the large hotels with their carefully trimmed lawns and orderly hedges. Maybe Jamaica should be left untamed. The wildness of the sea, the untrimmed trees and the encroaching bush gave the place character.

Kwame smiled to himself. Yes, perhaps something could happen here, something good. He stepped from the minibus onto the ground which was drenched with dew. He glanced at Carla behind him.

She was reaching to lift her bag from behind her seat.

"Here, let me take it for you," Akete said gently. Carla looked tired and worn in the dim light.

Sonia and Monica moved towards the door with their duffel bags in their hands. Martin walked behind them. One by one the passengers left the minibus. The four weeks had begun.

CHAPTER 2

Carla lay watching the light coming through the chinks in the faded drapes. She was still tired, but then they had come in pretty late, she had read before going to bed and even in bed she had found it difficult to sleep. It was being in a strange room alone, and the interminable lap lap of the waves against the sand outside. Now the morning was here and she looked forwards to seeing Plantation Plains, the excavation site. She knew a little of its history: that the estate had been in the hands of the same family since the 1700s and that it had been infamous for treating its slaves with especial cruelty.

It had been very difficult for the university to obtain permission to excavate the site. Now that the estate was more a cattle breeding farm than a sugar plantation, things had changed and the old machines and buildings that had housed the paraphernalia of a sugar estate had fallen into ruin. Many buildings had disappeared.

Now the old masters were among the marginalised. Though some still had money, they could no longer hold onto their particular church pews and their seats in government. The Governor General and the Prime Minister were black men and there was hardly one man of the old dominant race in parliament.

Carla had gone to the Institute of Jamaica library in Kingston and looked up the history of Plantation Plains. Now she would learn for herself. She knew that the results of this excavation would either verify or reject some of what was in the history books.

She got out of bed and stretched. Her exams came soon and then, she hoped, postgraduate studies overseas. She had to do well in this archaeology practical. This was a chance to put some of the theory that she had learnt into practice and gain good marks as a result. Professor Milton was a good teacher, but why did he stare at her so? She always felt uncomfortable under his gaze.

She liked the way he responded to her essays and that made her try hard each time she received a new topic. But it was embarrassing the way he constantly praised her in front of the other students in the class. He obviously liked her, but was there any more to it than this?

After bathing, putting on clean socks and a good strong pair of shoes, blue jeans and T shirt, Carla went down to breakfast. The bell had gone almost five minutes earlier. Most of the others were already in the dining room. Then the Professor entered.

"Morning, morning everybody."

"Morning Professor."

"Carla, you're looking good today. Did you sleep well?"

"Yes, Professor," Carla lied. "I slept well, thank you."

"Well, breakfast time. What have we got here? A feast! Callaloo, fried dumplings and fried plantains! David and Martin, you're about to enjoy a really good Jamaican breakfast at last. No more bacon and eggs. Well, come on. Let's eat! Lots of work today!"

The Professor settled down at a table with the Jamaican students. The two white students sat in the far corner of the room, away from the rest. Akete came in with the ital food he had prepared for himself. He did not use salt and so he had asked permission to use the kitchen, though the hotel provided the raw materials. Akete sat next to Carla. He glanced at her now and again as he shovelled the green bananas into his mouth.

"Akete, you really hungry, man," she said.

"I telling you," said Akete, "is a long time I man don't eat. I and I have to go through the whole night without a scrap of food. This hotel business not so good you know. Nothing like you' own house an you' own woman to cook for you. Seen?"

Martin looked at Akete as he ate hungrily, "Dreadlocks seems to be starving. Why doesn't he eat the same food as the rest of us?" he said in a low undertone to David, but there was a lull in the conversation and Akete heard the remark.

"I man eat my clean ital food, not Babylon food, but you white boys wouldn't understand that."

"Maybe we have to work out a little understanding these next four weeks," Professor Milton said quickly. Martin blushed as Akete gave him a long, hard look.

Carla's mouth was so full she could only chew and swallow. The callaloo was really nice. The orange juice was fresh and pure, and the plantains just right. She looked across the room and wondered how the Americans were liking the food. She thought it strange that they had not seen fit to sit with them at the long table. There was room for two or three more. Then she looked across at Kwame whom she had not noticed before this morning. He was seated in a far corner eating silently. He had scarcely looked up from his meal during the brief altercation.

After eating it was time to collect the gear and set off to the plantation. The Professor and Kwame supervised the packing of the equipment – gloves, shovels, string, mallets and a host of other things that would be needed for the day.

Professor Milton called the group together. "Hard work today. But before we go, let me assign you to your sites. Kwame wants to supervise the slaves' village site. Sonia and Monica, you go with him; Akete, you wanted to do that site too. David and Martin, you go on to the great house site. Carla, you will be with them. I will supervise that site. The great house site, if you remember, is situated on the high hill close to where the cattle pen now stands. The slaves' village site is closer to the water tanks, down in the valley away from the road. OK. Let's go."

They bundled into the land-rovers which set off slowly on the uneven road. The Professor watched as a peadove lifted its wings and flew. Another joined it. He smiled. It reminded him of when he was young and courting. Then everything had been so alive. He remembered his young undergraduate days in England. Then every woman had been a mystery and a potential mate. He wondered how he had managed to keep dedicated to his work when there were so many young and accessible white women around.

He had slept with one or two, had enjoyed their friendship and even contemplated marriage to one of them. But then he had thought of home, of the purpose of his education and the need to hold the sanctity of his race intact. He had been a radical before he left Jamaica, had espoused the teachings of Marcus Garvey, even though it had put his scholarship at risk.

In those days the confusions between his desires and what he felt they ought to be had often left him feeling alienated and angry, but he had found safe ground when he met Agnes, the daughter of a white theology lecturer at the university and his rather staid coloured wife. He had taken to going to visit this lecturer, who kept open house for the few overseas students at Oxford. He had found solace there, a safe haven from the pressures of his personal and academic life. The lecturer, who had taught both in Africa and the Caribbean, never talked theology, but discussed instead the life in the islands from which his own wife and the young history student had come. They had talked about how much of Africa still survived in the Caribbean and these discussions had often stilled the student's anger.

He had married Agnes because it seemed the most natural thing to do. He still loved her in his way. She had been the bedmate with whom he had been comfortable and a lifemate who was more a safe harbour than an exciting sea vessel. She had borne him three children, all now grown and away from home.

They were still happy together. She understood that he had to travel and regarded the urges he felt for other women if he stayed away from her too long with resigned tolerance.

Now some of the young women students that he taught were more than a little friendly towards him and he regarded this as a just reward for a job that paid relatively little. He gazed at Carla. It was always the ones who seemed most resistant to his charms who interested him the most. She was a challenge.

Carla stared in front of her at the wide band of asphalt. It was still cool, with dew on the grass. She had looked forward to this for months and hoped that nothing would spoil it for her. She thought of home for a while. There, too, the ground doves would fly upwards from the roads at one's approach. Whenever she went home she walked the lanes looking at the trees and shrubs and birds that flew about the branches. Then she would go back to her father and ask, *Which bird had that colour, which bird sounds like this*, and try to imitate their sounds. Her father, with his vast knowledge of country ways, could always tell her. She never ceased to marvel at him.

David sat beside the driver, chatting easily, praising his

skills as they passed the rough spots and began to climb the little slope towards the sites. He knew that Carla was sitting just behind him, leaning forward with her arms folded on the back of his seat. David felt close to her then, though by now he realised that he had a rival. Not much of a rival, though. The Professor was old; he was young.

As the other land-rover overtook them, Akete leaned out and shouted, "Hail de man! I an' I man gone ahead. See you!"

The driver grinned and shouted, "Is just because de Prof is here! You wait!"

By the time the Professor's land-rover arrived at the site, the dew was leaving the grass. Kwame was standing with his group under a star-apple tree where their driver sat chewing a blade of grass. Akete had climbed the tree, searching for ripe fruit.

David and Martin walked a little way up the hill and looked down at the group.

The driver removed the grass from his mouth and shouted, "Mind grass lice you know. Them plentiful roun' here!"

"That's all in the game, all in the game," Kwame muttered. "We'll all be picking off grass lice for months."

"True sah, true, but them love stranger. Is like mosquito. Me an' you now, dem don't bother wid we, but them love stranger."

"But, I am a stranger here too," said Kwame.

"Yes sah. But you look like we. You look like we."

Kwame didn't pursue this line of argument any further and they all began to unload the land-rovers. First there was grid-work to do before the actual digging began. Archaeologists from the University had already used a magnetometer to locate the best sites and draw large scale maps of the area. The Professor led his group up the hill to begin laying their grid.

Kwame led his group to the other side of the hill where they had found the site of the old slave village. Under his guidance they too began the grid work. The sun was hot and they had to rest frequently and seek shelter under the shade of the ancient star-apple trees which stood all around the site. Akete wondered if they had been there since slavery days. They seemed to stand like witnesses over them. They were also full of fruit and it was difficult for Akete to see them and not want to do something about his stomach. He was hungry again and all they had brought with them was clean drinking water. He would bring a sandwich the next day.

The group worked on. Slowly they prised the grass away from the soil. It was difficult and monotonous work. The earth was hard and littered with cattle droppings. The cattle had been moved to pastures on the other side of the property while the excavation was in progress.

There were few artefacts in the top layer of soil. They found a few tiny red beads and white beads on the slaves' village site; these were carefully sorted and put into labelled plastic bags. There were also pieces of white chalky-looking clay, the remains of pipes.

Kwame grunted as he picked one up and turned it over in hands. "This is the slaves' village all right," he said, "the plantation owners would hardly smoke from these. They would have used sophisticated wooden pipes from Britain."

"And these beads?" Akete asked as he rubbed off the red earth from around one of them.

"Remember your history, Akete? Beads were one of things used in exchange for slaves in Africa. They seem to have been prized by the Africans here too."

As it neared noon the sweat poured down their backs and from under their armpits. Akete still had the energy, though, to try to kill a centipede as it fled from its hiding place.

Kwame called out, "Don't kill it! It has a right to live too!"

"Why?" Akete asked, as the centipede found another hole.

"Only kill for food. We're not the only creatures on the face of the earth."

Akete looked at Kwame curiously. Centipedes stung and stung hard too, but because of his respect for African ways, he decided never to kill an insect on the site.

Lunchtime came and the group wandered off to join the others at the great-house site. Akete noted with satisfaction that the sun was turning the white men into lobsters. Carla was sifting through some soil, preoccupied. The Professor, stripped to the waist, showed a hairy chest that was flecked with grey like his beard.

All around them the trees grew firm and tall. There were pimento trees and wild tamarind trees. The pimento trees would bear tiny green berries to be picked later on in the year, then dried, cleaned and sold for export. The ripe fruit would be used to make pimento dram. Oil would sometimes be extracted from the leaves and the "steel bush", or leaves from which the oil had been taken, would often be bought by farmers to mulch their crops.

Carla recalled the days of pimento picking at home. Days of sitting under trees and listening to stories and jokes. Days of cooking dumplings, round and large and tough, eaten with codfish that was roasted still salty and hard.

She and the Professor watched the approach of the others from the slaves' village site.

"What, lunchtime already?" he asked.

"Yes Prof, lunchtime," said Kwame.

The Professor glanced at his watch and nodded.

"I thought you would be feeling the strain, Prof," said Kwame.

"Yes, I know I'm old. If you live to my ripe old age you won't even be able to handle a machete. You watch and see. Ask the girls. I'm as strong as an ox in spite of everything."

There were smiles on all their faces as they packed up to go back to the hotel for lunch. They would return afterwards to complete the day's work.

"It should be cooler at about three o'clock or so," said the Professor to David. "So let's get going. Carla, you look like a dedicated archaeologist already. Come along. You must be really hungry now. Save your strength for better times."

The jeeps moved more slowly over the hot asphalt. They were all hot and tired when they arrived back at the hotel.

CHAPTER 3

That evening, after returning from the site, the group gathered in a room at the other end of the hotel compound to learn more about the purpose of the excavation.

"Let's see the big fella perform now," Martin said as he and David walked to the lecture. David smiled.

"The big bloke was okay at the site," he said. "He was pleasant enough to us, and he works bloody hard."

"Like a black, eh," said Martin. "You know, he's got an eye on the girl."

"Which girl?"

"Carla."

"Her? I must admit she is kinda cute. She could be nice to get to know a little better. Don't you think so, Martin?"

"If you get lucky, kiddo, don't forget me. It could be kinda interesting. A cute little chick."

David was silent for a while. Then he said, "We will see what we will see. There are others around, you know. You're welcome to try them. But, let's hear what the Prof's got to say."

The students sat down as the professor took the stand. Akete sat near the doorway the better to slip out for a spliff. He badly needed one. Tension had been building up in him all day. There had been that stupid remark by one of the white boys, and though the trip was important to him, he felt restricted in this company. They were mostly young, middle-class kids. He had his woman and daughter waiting at home and here he was in this hotel. It was a bit too comfortable for comfort. And those white boys; their presence on the dig felt like an intrusion into something private. For some reason, it all took him back to his childhood days, a childhood of privilege. He had long ago divorced his parents and made himself part of the sufferer's culture, but now he felt tempted to give his daughter a little bit of the Babylon that he had experienced. He had been well cared for as a child, had helpers in the kitchen to cook for him and gardeners to keep the outdoors immaculately clean. Sheba attended a large, overcrowded primary school. She knew what he had never known as a child: what it was like to be hungry, to be without good strong clothing and regarded as lacking potential and possibility.

He knew that the values that went with the material comforts his mother and father had showered on him had crippled his appreciation of his own people. He had not known the real culture of the countryside that he now often visited for spiritual renewal, nor could he have dreamed that Trench Town was to be the place to experience his own joy. He knew hunger and deprivation, but he also knew the love of his woman and happiness whenever he saw his child. But he still felt guilty about having lived a life of privilege when he saw the pain around him. But when he heard the women laugh and the men chuckle, and heard the children sing, even as they played close to the garbage heaps, he knew the power of the human spirit. In the rich world of Babylon, he had never really known love. He knew now that love did not come with ease, but deeply, with a knife wound that touches the heart.

Carla sat with her notebook in her hands and stared out through the door. Outside the peenie wallies flew. The only lights in the grounds came from the hotel's windows. The lone dog guarding the hotel barked nervously, and in the distance the waves came and went, came and went against the sand. An owl hooted in the distance. For Carla the place had a beautiful wildness. She felt that nature needed no one to order her affairs. Give her a free hand and she was a perfect gardener: a polished preserver, a selective destroyer and an accomplished builder on the ruins of the old. But just at present, Carla felt restless and diminished. She felt that too much of her life had been about absorbing knowledge, not living it. At home she had been sheltered and it was in books that she had found her escape. But she loved her family, loved her home and the surrounding countryside, the people who rode donkeys or drove rickety trucks, whose culture was an inexplicable mixture of stiff Englishness and more moving, fluid African ways.

She had listened to the drumbeats of the pocomania bands and attended the church in which a Scotsman preached, had visited the home of an old medicine woman and had seen the white doctor in the town with her ailments. Each had its own place, its own time. As a child she had scarcely thought about it, but now, what did they mean, the two bloods, the two traditions, which flowed in her veins?

The Professor started to speak about the relationship between archaeology and other sources of history and how each could throw light on the other. How it was possible to trace the history of Plantation Plains back to the land grants made to Lt. Robert Francis in 1670, because these documents had been held by the old Jamaican Assembly. Francis had been a soldier-adventurer who had come with the army of General Venables to take Jamaica from the Spanish. It was possible to trace additions of land to the estate because these, too, were recorded in legal documents. It was probable, in the light of contemporary reports that, in the earliest decades of the estate's existence, capital had been accumulated through hunting cattle and wild boar, and that the land had gradually been cleared with the help of small numbers of slaves. It was known from the records kept by the Francis family, and now in the Institute of Jamaica, that sugar cultivation had begun in the early eighteenth century, that the estate house had been built in 1730, and that by 1760 the estate had employed three hundred and two slaves. All this was recorded, even the names of the slaves and their age at purchase. But so much was unknown, and it was here that archaeology could throw more light on the past. Had there been any surviving Amerindian groups when the Francis family settled the area? Had there been any contact, any exchange of materials between the Amerindians and the African slaves?

Akete thrust forward his hand. "Professor Milton, isn't it true that Africans came to the New World long before Columbus and slavery, and mixed with the people here?"

"Van Sertima has written a book arguing that idea," the Professor replied, "but I can't say I'm convinced by the theory, however pleasing it would be to believe it."

"I've never heard of that," Martin said. "Wasn't it the Vikings who first discovered the Americas?"

"Vikings!" Akete sprang. Blasted white bastard, trying to belittle black people. "Who says Vikings come here first? When Vikings and Europeans sitting down to eat cow dung as meat, Africans came here. The Amerindians knew about the Africans. The Amerindian dem know more 'bout Africa than 'bout Europe. And may I intrude a point of reference, that the African bredda never destroy de Amerindian culture. Is oonu do that. When Africans had universities, Europeans lived in huts!"

"Akete, you're mixing up historical theories for which there's good evidence and beliefs for which there is no concrete proof," said the professor.

"Belief? If is something that we just believe, then all the artefacts we find here will not be concrete evidence? It will just be belief? What we come here for? To build up belief like we build up religion? I thought archaeology was advanced enough to provide proof, good substantial proof, not just belief!" Akete was really angry now.

Carla closed her notebook. The twins watched open-mouthed. David's neck was red. Martin fumbled with his pen. Akete's eyes flashed with anger. He didn't expect the professor to counter him like that. As black men they ought to be fighting together to win the ultimate battle. It was time to mash up Babylon, time for redemption song. Free our minds of the hogwash, clean our souls of the white massa shit. Then build. Build again black man's pride.

"That is why Babylon still rule," he said quietly. "We doan know we own history, we own culture. Babylon must burn but we haffi find we own soul. We have to find we own Zion before we find the truth. When we a go find we self, Professor? When we a go know de truth?"

Kwame heard the agony in Akete's voice. His plight was one he thought he understood. As a western-trained Ghanaian he had known something of the same divisions, though he had a language, a tribe and a proud past to sustain him. Here was Akete trying to find a route back in a society which denied its African roots. The road back was potholed and still strewn with the rubble of the past.

When Kwame spoke, his voice was like a balm. "Akete, we have to learn to accept ourselves as we are, what we have been, the changes we have gone through and what we are becoming."

"You right," Akete said quietly. "We have fe stop try to please the white man, but to please weself. We have fe stop copy everything de white man do, but do things fe please weself. That is when we will come into we own."

Kwame continued, "I don't think you're hearing all that I'm saying, Akete. It's that if we learn to love our own homes, our own buildings, our own art, our own music, our own psyches as they have become through time – with discrimination, of course – then we'll be able to live comfortably together with others – white, black, pink or blue."

Martin piped up, his small, quick voice staccato in the room. "Don't you think that Western culture has made the world a better place?"

"Better than what and for whom?" asked the Professor.

"But, but, for everybody."

"The West has not made it a more moral place and it is certainly not a safer, cleaner place to live. Europe conquered with the whip, the word and the weapon. What I call the three W's. They have discarded the whip of slavery for the whip of the market. They have discarded the whip of the word for the whip of political ideology. And they have replaced the old, intimate weapons with the technology of the nuclear bomb. We still have the whip on our backs, Martin!"

"But what of Western technology, sir," Martin said. "What about medicine? And scientific discoveries, better food, more knowledge and all of that?"

"There has to be a balance in this world. When the scales tip too far in one direction we lean towards destruction. There is a delicate balance between good and evil, order and energy, light and darkness, the world of spirit and the world of matter. Sometime the scale tips towards evil and darkness, sometimes towards goodness and light. If we allow the scientific method and all the paraphernalia of science to control us without moving towards say, the spiritual world, the moral world, we upset the balance, and the scales will tip us towards destruction. We must maintain a balance. Now we have an imbalance. Technology without moral and ecological responsibility has created that imbalance. We're destroying ourselves. But these are issues more relevant to tomorrow's lecture which will deal with the relationship between slavery and capitalist development and particularly the history of Plantation Plains. Let me return to the subject of archaeology and what we can learn from the excavations we have just begun..."

Akete sat and listened. He was silent now. Martin sat looking like a hurt child. David listened keenly but his neck was still red. It was as though a small grenade had exploded in the room.

When the lecture ended and they went back to their rooms. Carla felt that there was a chasm stretching deep and wide. She was afraid that it would make the next four weeks painful to live through. Why had the white boys come, and why was Akete so provocative?

Later, as she lay in her bed she thought of David and the Professor, but especially of David. There was something about the young white man that appealed to her even though she resented the attention he paid her. But he was white. She was black. There was no future there. But David had blushed deep. His seemed an earnestness not to provoke but to inquire into, to investigate. The Professor's words had come with a finality and a sharpness that cut deep. She did not, though, question their truth.

The Professor was an old man now. Carla wondered about his youth and why he had waited so long to come home. What of his wife? Had she been pretty? Did the Professor still love her? Was his interest in her just a passing fancy? She knew all about his reputation as a womaniser. As she lay there a feeling like bile rose in her. She twisted and turned and sighed deeply. It was some time before she was able to sleep.

She woke to find sunlight streaming through her window. Swiftly she bathed and dressed, wondering if the others had already left and why they had not roused her. She went downstairs to find them at breakfast.

"Morning Carla," said the Professor, peering at her over his glasses.

"Morning Professor."

"Morning, morning," she said to everyone else as she sat down. She was really very hungry. Yesterday had made her ravenous and now she felt a few aches and pains in her muscles. She was not much used to outdoor work. "A book-worm in a room," her father had often called her. "Get out and meet people and enjoy yourself," but she had remained in her room. Her move to the university had just been a change of four walls, a bed and a few other pieces of furniture.

It was rundown for breakfast, and the salted mackerel seasoned in coconut milk and the soft, cooked green bananas melted in Carla's mouth.

"Good food this," Martin mumbled.

It was then that Carla realised that Akete was not around. "Where's Akete?"

"Cooking his ital food as usual," Sonia replied.

"So late?" Carla asked.

"I think he went for a swim last night," said Kwame.

"Mnnm," said Carla as she dug her fork into a soft green banana finger.

CHAPTER 4

It was a quiet day on Plantation Plains with everyone working and little time for rest. There was an air of studied politeness in the group, as though all were trying hard to be on good terms with each other so that the dig would not be disrupted by the differences between them. The Professor continued to treat everyone exactly as he had done before: *Carla this, Martin that, David have a look at this*.

On the slave village site Kwame seemed even more thoughtful than usual, a quiet smile on his face. Akete sat under a tree eating a star-apple slowly, as though he was trying to drag out the joy from its soft, succulent flesh. A mockingbird came down beside him, picked at an insect in the grass and looked at him as if to say, *Who are you and what do you think you are doing?*

Akete looked startled as the bird made off for the tamarind tree that stood on the hill.

"Birds," he wondered aloud. "Where dem come from?"

"They're the descendants of dinosaurs," said Kwame.

"Dinosaurs? But de descendants of dinosaurs are lizards."

"No Akete, birds are." There was a smile in Kwame's voice. "It's not surprising that people think it was lizards since we have an idea of what dinosaurs looked like and there is a resemblance. Still, no one can ever be certain about anything. There is that old quarrel between Darwin and God, or rather those who claim to know God. We know nothing. We know nothing of the past, Akete. We can only hope we know. That is the fact of history."

"But some things are there to be seen, Kwame," said Sonia.

"We interpret things depending on our frame of reference, our own past, our own mindset. We see, but what we see is not necessarily what could be seen or interpreted, and that is the point. That we can never completely know the past is the only 'fact' that we do know."

Akete sat on the grass and thought about this for a while. He found Kwame most interesting. Like yesterday when he had been about to kill the centipede. Now this. Akete got up from the grass. A startled nightingale flew upwards. Akete grinned to himself, got up and joined the others.

As they moved down the slope towards the land-rovers at the end of the day, the Professor walked beside Carla. He turned and smiled at her.

"Tired?" he asked.

"Exhausted, Professor."

"What are you doing tonight?"

"Studying first, then maybe I'll read a book. *Grapes of Wrath*. I've been really enjoying it."

"Why don't you relax for a while? There's always a disco. This is the north coast, you know. We can all go out and enjoy ourselves. How about it?"

"I'm not sure I'd like a disco. Thanks Professor, but no."

"Then what do you like? Don't you like company?"

"Yes, I do like company sometimes but discos. No thanks."

"Oh come on, Carla, ease up. You need to relax. Come with us to the disco." He put a restraining hand on her arm.

"Well," she hesitated, "maybe... just maybe... I'll think about it, Professor Milton."

"Good," he smiled at her. "I know you'll come. Give *Grapes of Wrath* a rest for this evening."

"Well... Okay, Professor."

He smiled again. Maybe he would have a chance with this girl. She needed to be pulled from that shell of hers. She needed to see the world, and who was a better teacher than himself? He had seen the world. And he was sure she was a little attracted to him, maybe not sexually yet, but that would come.

David had been watching. What had the Professor been saying to Carla? He decided that if he wanted to get anywhere with her he needed to start soon. He knew it would not be easy. He was beginning to realise that his colour might be more of a disadvantage than an advantage in this case. But he was growing to like Carla very much. She was so quiet, but there was something about her that made him want to know her. It was as if she had a mystery hidden somewhere that he wanted to unravel.

That night the Professor would give his second lecture before they went to the disco. After a meal of fried chicken and rice and peas, potato salad and soursop juice, they all went down to what had become known as the lecture hall.

"I wonder if sparks will fly again tonight?" said Sonia to Carla as they walked together.

"I hope not," said Carla.

"Why not? I loved last night!" said Monica. "The Prof has such deep knowledge; so has Kwame, and Akete has such spirit. The Americans came out a weak fourth if you ask me."

"I don't think so entirely," Carla said, as though to herself.

She turned to Sonia who had paused to wipe some mud from her shoes.

"What you mean, you don't think so?" Sonia asked.

"I disagree totally with Martin's view of history, but what if Europe had never entered Africa or the Americas? Where would we be now? What would the world be like? Would Africa be a heaven? I think we somehow have to learn to see something beneficial in all change, in spite of the pain that comes with it."

The lights in the lecture room were on. Professor Milton was already there, arranging his lecture notes on a rickety table. Kwame was sitting in the corner and Akete close to the door. David and Martin came in behind the three girls.

Professor Milton told them that he was going to talk about the changes in European economic structures that brought industrial sugar production to the Plantation Plains Estate. The Caribbean plantations, he told them, were among the very first steps in the development of Western capitalism and its basis in accumulation and industrial production and its commoditisation of both labour and the objects which craftsmen had once made for use rather than profit. Eric Williams's *Capitalism and Slavery* charted that connection with great mastery as long ago as 1943. He paused for a moment. "We have," he said, "to study this process with all our historian's care for evidence and detail. But we can't forget that these economic processes have a moral dimension. What does Williams say somewhere? 'When things are in the saddle...'" Then his voice lowered and he seemed to be speaking, not as the scholar quoting sources, but from somewhere deep inside himself.

"Europe destroyed civilisations and cultures in order to feed its own ego. It did it with the myth that Europeans were God's loved ones and all others were infidels without a God.

It did it to feed its stomach and to build a civilisation. It did it to establish the so-called superiority of the white man and the so-called inferiority of all other peoples. It did it to secure a place at the head of the international scheme of things and in order to control the world. It did this believing that what it was doing was right. The religious fervour that lingered after the fall of the middle ages and the brief renewals of that fervour by evangelists in the 17th and 18th centuries made Europe believe that it was the force to civilise the world and bring enlightenment to its peoples."

The company sat and listened. The night was still. The lap lap of the waves on the seashore was a soothing, soft punctuation in the stillness of the night. The Professor's voice seemed louder than it was. He spoke almost in a whisper, yet they all heard him.

"How often we hear of Indian savages. How often we hear of African backwardness. How often we hear of Europe's influence in glowing terms and of all other races disparagingly. But Europe erred when it destroyed, for Europe had little of its own to offer in the end. The wisdom of the Greeks and the organising ability of the Romans had, of course, left their mark. But basically, the European can be seen as a barbarian, one who destroys the civilisations he encounters. The European replaces the natural civilisation of the world with the barbarity of technology. If science had been used only to advance the good of the world, what a wonderful place this would be, but what we have is technology without an ethical framework, controlled only by the market. Modern medicine has lengthened life but it is threatening to play God with our genes. The weapons sold by the West to their clients in the developing world destroy those whom medical science lets through the net. The people who pollute this world are not the Africans or the Indians but the high-living, gasoline-flaunting consumers of the industrialised West. When Europe built, it destroyed."

The Professor paused. The air grew heavy in the room. The movement of the moths around the single light bulb in the ceiling drew Monica's attention for a while.

"Who flings out the garbage from their own neighbourhoods into other people's backyards because they don't yet count for anything in the markets of the world? Who cares? The Nazarene has been replaced by the bottom line. We worship the figures in the bank book. The larger the figure the greater the god."

Akete's chair scraped the floor as he leaned forwards, the better to catch the Professor's words. Outside the peenie wallies flew as if there were no stars, no moon, no electric lights to light the nightfarer's way. But Akete did not see them. His eyes were on the Professor.

"Ancient civilisations lived with nature. The European today lives outside of nature and is perturbed that he cannot altogether tame it. We have their nuclear weapons, we have chemical warfare and we have the European version of the grin. This is the way the European seeks to show his teeth when he wishes to patronise. The grin is a grin because it does not involve his eyes. He gave us all the notion of the salvation of the soul which he claimed he learned from the Nazarene. Then he abandoned the soul in the cathedrals of the middle ages and now worships his own technological power, his own ego, his own weapons."

Martin sat astonished, his face red with anger, his teeth clenched. How dare he? Jesus Christ! How dare he?

"But Europe has given black people a gift," the Professor continued. "It put in their way an obstacle. We have been less than human in the European scheme of things, but we have also been given a mountain to climb. The higher the mountain, the higher you climb, the further you reach. The greatest people in this world are those who have had to fight against the odds. When they break through the barriers that confront them, they are truly triumphant. Thank God for the obstacle."

Martin thought of walking out. David felt embarrassed. Akete sat with mouth slightly open, his eyes gleaming. Kwame sat calmly as though drinking in sweet palm wine. Carla listened with intensity, loving every word. The twins were glowing with pride.

For an hour the Professor spoke with scarcely more than the occasional pause. He kept his voice low and his eyes shone as he spoke. It was almost nine o'clock when he ended. When he invited questions and comments, Martin was the first to speak.

"Professor Milton," he said, "Your message is one-sided. What is the European version of the grin? How different is it from the black man who grins while he kills? Or the black judge who judges harshly because the defendant is white?"

"How often do we hear the tales of that sort, Martin? Isn't it rather that we hear too often of some black man beaten or even murdered by the police? You have never entered a department store in the USA and been trailed because you are black, have you?"

"No," Martin replied, "but don't you think that the West's technology and science has given the world untold possibilities? Look at the economic miracles in the Far East. Sure, there is suffering, but isn't that inevitable when great changes take place?"

"Yes, that's what the missionaries tried to teach the slaves. Sure, they were suffering, but it was for their own good. They would get their reward for obedience later. For the time being they had to turn the other cheek. That's what the Europeans taught us. We turned the other cheek and they delivered us another slap in the face. Slavery, mutilation, the whip and then our minds. They took our land and warped our minds."

"As Bob Marley sang, *Liberate yourself from mental slavery, None but ourselves can free our minds*," Akete said.

"Yes, Akete. Yes," the Professor answered.

Kwame turned to Martin. "You picture the white nations as more advanced than us, Martin?" he asked, his voice soft and easy.

"Well yes. The evidence is there."

"I think you're looking at the issue from too narrow a perspective. You don't acknowledge the history of the world outside or before the rise of Europe. You judge only on the basis of economics and technology. Aren't the ecologists of your own world teaching us that we have to build on other, more human values? You need to learn from those who live with nature, or nature will make all of us pay. You deny what you have appropriated in the past, and even now your country cannot acknowledge what its culture owes to African Americans. But I think it is you who are becoming the mimics now. Isn't American culture, even in language, following the lead of African American innovation? Don't I see white rastamen and white reggae artists?"

"All human beings copy each other," Martin said. "The tiniest baby mimics its mother."

"But it's what the Europeans and Americans have done with the cultures they borrowed from. Yes, much of Europe's knowledge was copied from the Indians, from the Egyptians, from the Chinese, from the Arabs, and yes, from the Africans north of the Sahara. You mimic and pretend to improve what you mimic. You turned Chinese fireworks into gunpowder. A significant change in use, I think."

"I don't agree entirely with Martin," David said. "But isn't it true that all men fight?"

"But in the history of the world, has any race killed as many as the white race?" Sonia asked.

"All men crave power," said David again.

"Yes, but has any race pursued power over others with as much single-minded ruthlessness as the white races of the world?"

The night noises broke over the silence that descended on the room, and when the discussion continued, the tone became less angry. Though there was neither agreement nor acceptance of the others' views there was more willingness to give space to them.

Carla went to her room after the lecture. She was part of the silence that had descended at the end of the session. For the first time she'd heard a different voice within her, a quiet, still voice. She'd listened and marvelled. She needed solitude, a time to think, to reach the soul inside her that had been bared that night, the black soul, the Zion soul. But for now she also needed the company of the group and she was glad it had been decided that they were all going to a disco that night.

As she sat in her room before getting ready to go out, she wondered where David really stood on these issues. She had to admire Martin's courage, or was it just arrogance, in sticking to his point of view in this company. When David kept quiet, what did he really think? Was he just trying to sit on the fence, and give no offence to anyone? If that was so he was pretty spineless.

Carla combed her hair and smoothed out her dress, admiring for a moment her reflection in the mirror. Her heart began to beat a little faster.

CHAPTER 5

The streets were full of people and the night was warm when they arrived in Ocho Rios. The smell of food was in the air as the restaurants and the streetside vendors of pan chicken, hot dogs, buns and cheese vied for tourist trade, along with the gaudily dressed prostitutes. They stopped outside a club from which green, red and blue lights flashed at intervals and loud, insistent, music throbbed out into the night.

The buzz of voices continued for a while as they entered the club, and then there was silence. The white faces of well-dressed men and women inside turned to look at the group. David, Martin, Kwame and Carla were already through the door. Akete, always impatient to be doing whatever there was to be done, was attempting to go in. He was blocked by a big burly security guard, black and clean shaven.

"You cyan' enter!"

"Why not?" asked Akete.

"You ent properly dressed."

"Listen man, cut de shit. I coming in."

The big man continued to block Akete's path.

The Professor, who had been somewhat behind Akete, stepped forward.

"Yes sir?" the guard asked respectfully, though he towered over the Professor.

"What's the matter?" the Professor asked mildly.

"This man ca...ca...cannot enter!"

"Why not?"

"He ent properly dressed!"

The proprietor appeared. "What's the problem?" he asked with forced cheerfulness as he approached.

"This man," the doorman said, pointing to Akete, "wants to come in."

The proprietor summed up the situation in a glance, taking in Akete's dashiki and long dreadlocks. "Fucking ghetto scum," he said under his breath, "come to mash up the evening."

"Yes sir," he addressed the Professor, his voice bright and brittle. "What can I do for you?"

"We just want to come in..." the Professor kept his voice low, but emphasised every syllable.

The Americans waited in the semi-dark room. The two girls watched with concern; Kwame looked on in amazement. Akete's anger grew.

"I'm afraid I can't allow that. You see," the proprietor pointed to Akete, "he's not properly dressed."

"What's wrong with him?"

"Well, the clothes... they're just not appropriate."

"His clothes or his hairstyle?" asked the Professor.

"You see, sir," said the proprietor, "we often get raided. The rastaman cannot come in here. Let me remind you that I decide who enters my establishment."

"You do?" asked the Professor. "Isn't this is a public place that we should be able to enter without interference?"

"A public place?" the proprietor's voice rose in pitch. "This is my place. I decide who is to enter."

"And what do you now decide?" the Professor asked.

"That this man cannot enter!"

Akete found his voice: "Cyan enter? Who de fuck say I man cyan enter?"

"I do!" The proprietor said.

"We'll see about that," the Professor said. "We'll see what happens when I report you to the tourist board."

The Professor turned and went. The group followed.

"Fucking intellectuals," the proprietor muttered to himself as he watched them leave. "Think they own the whole fucking world."

David muttered to Martin, "Christ, there's prejudice even between black people here."

Martin grinned. "So Akete defends his own and his own reject him." Akete overheard.

"You shut your trap too, you piece of pork! You watch your step. I man going to deal with you!" He spat the words out over his shoulder and walked quickly ahead of the group.

Akete walked ahead on his own wondering why he had not fought the rass claat man at the club. Was he losing his spirit? Did he need the Prof to defend him? He needed a spliff. He fingered his back pocket nervously. He dared not smoke one here.

The feelings of panic that sometimes came on cold grey evenings and rainy, thought-filled nights rushed into him. It was the frightening realisation that in the world of the powerful, he was still a child. Although he had read a lot, his learning seemed to him now to be unfocused, incomplete, totally wanting in substance. Yet he was growing old. He had a child. He had his woman but had gone to study at the University because child and woman were not enough, and he longed for knowledge. He respected the Professor's eloquence and his cool exterior, but where had it got them?

Akete's silence grew and budded in the minds of the others, but they said little. Kwame muttered under his breath, his anger coming in spurts. It was he who broke the silence.

"That fucking semi-black proprietor and that stinking ass-sucking black doorman! They betray us. That is what they do. They both knew what they were doing tonight. The black security guard was doing it for cash and security and that semi-black bastard for his skin. Traitors, both of them. "

Monica mumbled something about finding somewhere else and Martin agreed. No one seemed to hear them. The Professor's silence lay like a blanket of rotting leaves on the company.

It was Sonia who spoke out loudly enough for all to hear. "Let's find another place and forget about all this."

"Yes," Monica said quickly, "let's not spoil the evening."

They walked towards the main street and turned into a little cafe, where they ordered beers. But there was no room for conversation, no room even for the slightest bit of chit chat. The people at the tables around them seemed to notice the silence which hung over the group like a dull cloak. Suddenly the Professor said, "Let's call it a night. The evening is spoilt already. I will write to the tourist board about this. They won't get away with it!"

They returned to the hotel in almost complete silence. Carla sighed with relief as they entered the compound. She was thoughtful, her eyes lowered. As they walked back to their rooms, David was beside her. Their arms brushed. Carla looked up and slipped slightly on the dew-damp grass. David reached out and steadied her. He smiled down at her.

Akete, seeing this, muttered angrily and spat.

The Professor said, "Carla, be careful. Watch your step."

"In more ways than one," Monica murmured as they walked through the open door into the lobby.

CHAPTER 6

Carla woke the next morning feeling as though the world was her palace. It was slightly cool with a hint of rain in the air. She hoped, though, that it would not rain as she wanted to work on the site all day. Then she remembered what had happened at the disco the night before. She had thought about it before going to sleep. The feelings of bewilderment and hurt returned. She felt so angry about what had happened to Akete, but it wasn't as simple as that. The prejudice he faced as a dreadlocked rasta was wrong, but would *she* have ever dreamt of taking anyone like Akete home to meet her parents? She knew what her father's response would be, and though she wished he was more open-minded, how could she stop loving and respecting him. Then there had been the angry exchange between Akete and Martin. She understood why Akete had been so aggressive. Martin was a tactless fool, but hadn't there been some truth in what he said? And what of Kwame's angry outburst when he'd called the nightclub owner a semi-black bastard? Was that what he thought of someone like her too? Then there'd been the brief encounter with David as they entered the hotel. It had been innocent enough. So what was she to make of Monica's comment? For a moment she wished she was back at home, away from all this pressure, but then she told herself off for being so feeble.

By the time they arrived at the estate that morning, both her agitation and the clouds had melted away again and the sun beat down over everything. She had always loved the sun; it relaxed her and made her feel happy. She could see why the Aztecs loved and worshipped it.

She looked at the star-apple trees on the hill and then at the sun again. It was true what the Professor had said. Primordial man's instinct was to respect or even worship nature. Industrial man looked to tame it or subordinate it to his will. Because he could understand some aspects of nature and control or at least predict some of its whims, he began to play God and now he was destroying the world.

There were birds everywhere, in the trees, in the grass, along the path that she was now following. The ground doves rose when she came close, only to come back to the same spot as soon as she had passed. She was first to arrive at the site.

"Carla," someone called. It was the Professor, loping towards her. "Why are you in such a hurry, my dear?"

His face was blank except for his eyes, which hinted at a little mockery, a little playfulness that Carla immediately reacted to. What was this man about? She frowned, then she closed her shell around her like a clam and said coolly, "I want to get on with the work."

"What did you think of last night?" he asked.

Carla thought for a while before answering then said, "Professor Milton, what's wrong with us? Why do we treat each other so badly?"

"Why indeed, Carla. I fear it's because some of us still need to see ourselves reflected in the blue-eyed sea of the white man's eyes."

"But that's so silly."

"It is, isn't it? Only constant vigilance on our part and time will change that. I fear I won't live to see this nonsense gone forever, Carla, but I pray that you'll see it gone before you get too old."

Carla was silent. As they walked towards the great house site the Professor's hand brushed hers. She pulled her hand away and looked up. There was a flicker of anger on her face, but he was looking ahead of him and did not seem to have noticed her reaction.

David stood and watched them arriving side by side.

"So that's it," he muttered to himself. "Perhaps Carla would rather secure a good grade than be my friend." His bitter thoughts surprised him.

Akete saw the anger on David's face. He had observed the Professor's interest in Carla and decided he had to protect her from both men. He was certainly not interested in her for himself. He already had his own baby mother and his own child. Carla was a good girl. He would hate to see her used by either of the two men – by a womaniser nearly three times her age or a white boy looking for something exotic. Maybe he had to drop Carla a hint.

That day no rain fell. The sun grew hot and soon sweat was pouring from them. Carla worked hard. She was excited when she unearthed a piece of pottery that seemed to be part of an old vase. David photographed it before it was removed. The markings were different from any Carla had ever seen. The Professor looked at it closely.

"Mmmn. Now we're getting there," was all he said.

Carla placed the fragment in a plastic bag and labelled it. David came close to her. He smiled at her and said, "It's a lovely piece, isn't it?"

Carla looked at him. "Yes. What do you think it is?"

"It might be a piece of Delft china. Why do you like what we're doing so much, Carla? You seem so taken with it you hardly have time to speak to anyone."

Carla glanced at him. "I've never thought about it," she said. "I just like what I'm doing and I do it. I'm not hurting anyone am I?"

He smiled. "No. It's hard to imagine you hurting anyone." They continued in silence for a moment.

David searched for something to say. "Do you have a pet at home, Carla? Or anyone you care for a lot?"

"Yes, I've got a dog, but what's that got to do with anything?"

"Nothing much. But I was just thinking about Ben, my dog at home, and how much I miss him."

David looked at Carla as she tied the mouth of the plastic bag and picked up her shovel.

"At the end of all this, will you miss the rest of us?"

"I guess I will. After all, four weeks can seem a long time."

"But you scarcely talk to us, Carla."

"Well, you don't talk to me much either."

"Maybe we should get to know each other a little better."

"Maybe," Carla replied, but she had already bent down to resume her digging.

The Professor had seen the two young people talking and had to admit to himself that he felt jealous. So that was it! David was young and white. He was old. He had grey hair in his beard and on his head. If there was anything he hated about himself, it was his age. Oh, his looks were all right. He knew he looked distinguished with his greying beard and well-kept frame. But he was old and he knew it. His wife, though younger than himself, was also growing old. He hated the idea of growing frail and bent, of talking quietly to other old people in biblical verses about death and dying, of attending the funerals of old friends who had started going one by one. After every funeral he came back with fear in his heart. Who next, Lord?

Sure he was in his sixties. He had reached retirement age but had refused to retire and sit at home while the world still turned and while there was still so much to do. But he was also growing tired. He felt lost, abandoned. He felt the urge for youth and vitality and he wanted Carla. His wife no longer needed him. She had retired from creaking bedsprings and now read her biblical verses with greater absorption than ever. Now he wanted to initiate this girl into the real world. She lived in a dream.

They left the site earlier that day because of the heat and because everyone was so tired. The lecture was postponed.

That night, after the meal, the twins invited Carla to their room, eager to discuss the happenings of the night before and just hang out for a while. They shared peanuts and potato chips around while they chatted.

"What amazed me most," said Sonia, "was Akete. He said almost nothing until we'd left that place."

"But why?" Carla asked. "He's usually so vocal in class."

"As though him frighten of somet'ing," said Monica. "Big man like that! Him have to have the Prof speak for him, would you believe that? Him who smoke him spliff whenever him feel like it, let the Prof speak for him."

"There's a soft part to Akete. Maybe his outside shell is like glass. Breakable."

"Maybe. The Prof is strong though. He stood up like a man."

"We all follow him like puppy dog. That is the Prof for you. I never see it so, believe me," Sonia grinned at the memory.

"But what good will writing to the tourist board do," said Monica. "Kwame was mad, though. He cussed a word or two."

"You think he's never seen anything like that before?" Carla asked.

"I don't know," Sonia said. "I figure there would be people like that night club owner in Ghana. People who would kiss the white man's ass and turn against their own kind."

"Yes," Monica agreed. "Yes, I guess so. Everywhere the white man go him plant the root of his own superiority. Like some blasted kind of a demigod. And the black man will kill for him. Kill even his own kind."

"Divide and rule. The white man's maxim," Sonia said. "And we lap it up like puppy dogs who are at last 'civilised'. Black curse black, just like how black make big show of cursing white and then turn around and kiss him ass. The only problem is few black men will kiss another black man's ass, especially if they blacker than them."

"And if a black man mek it in the world, we same one turn around and kill him. Cause we all feel him cyan mek it by honest means. Him have to t'ief it, plant ganja for it, or go to foreign to clean toilets for it. There is no such thing as an honourable black man."

"The only honourable black man in the Third World psyche is the black man who has been recognised as such in the white world. Like Bob Marley. Is either that or we wait till them kill him off before them call him national hero. Like Sam Sharpe and Paul Bogle and Nanny," Monica continued.

"You know, even though Garvey had a large following, my father tell me the man was hated in some districts, and every man that follow him was a radical to be cut down. 'That black man don't know him place,' the old people used to say. Like Garvey should be like all of them. Lap they tail like puppy dog and eat leftovers."

"Like every other race on earth is united except the black race. Chiny man help Chiny man, Indians clannish, white man defend white man, only black people hate and betray one another so," said Sonia.

"I been hearing the same tale since I have sense" Carla said. "But you know, the whole human race have its ambiguities. White man kill white man too. Chiny man kill Chiny man."

"Yes I know that," Monica said. "And that is true. But how many Chiny man will kill another Chiny man for a Nigger. You tell me that. You tell me that, I say."

Nobody answered her. For a moment there was silence in the room. Sonia lay back on her bed. Carla put her hands behind her head and leaned back, at ease after the tension of the previous night.

"We need unity," she said, "and nobody has been able to get it into our heads, under our skins, anywhere it really matters. We are like divided tribes without leadership."

"Until the philosophy that holds one man superior and another inferior..." Sonia began to quote Bob Marley.

"You right you know, Sonia" said Monica quietly, "you right. We do it because we don't believe in weselves. We believe that God curse us and that we must be slave and live inferior lives. We hate we own culture and we own skin. Good hair and bad hair go with it."

"Yes," said Sonia as she stopped singing. "Yes, we believe we are small. So we will always be small, till we begin to learn the real truth about ourselves..."

That night Carla consulted her Zion self again. She heard the distant music of a reggae band, heard the deep boom boom of the drums, heard the voice that soared outward into the night, heard the pain of Burning Spear as he sang his song against the wind.

CHAPTER 7

Next day the rain poured. The students woke up dreading a long boring day, perhaps spent listening to the Professor in the lecture room. David thought of Carla alone in her room and the Professor thought of starting to classify the artefacts.

Carla bathed in very cold water and then went down to breakfast. It was pouring so hard outside that it was difficult to hear anyone speak above the din. They sat and ate slowly. Akete came in with a bowl of oatmeal and a glass of peanut-flavoured milk. David moved across to Carla who was staring out through the window at the torrents of rain.

"Carla," he half whispered, "how about a session together today? Maybe you could tell me something about this country. Let's ditch archaeology for a while. I don't have a clue what Jamaica is all about."

"What do you want to know? You can't learn much about Jamaica in one little conversation!"

"Well, there could be others, I guess. I want you to tell me about the people of this country. I'd really like to know."

"OK. Maybe. Let's hear what the Prof has to say first."

The wind was still high but the rain was lessening now. Professor Milton shouted across the room, "As soon as there's a break we'll go to the big room. I'd like us to sort the artefacts and come to some conclusions about what we've found so far."

They all groaned.

"Couldn't we have a free day, Prof? We've worked really hard so far." Martin looked hopeful as he said this. The Professor ignored him. "After that Kwame will show us some of the slides he brought from Ghana."

"OK!" Akete shouted. "I an I man would like to see that."

At last they were able to made their way across the sodden grass to the lecture room. Slowly they arranged the tables and put the plastic bags of artefacts into groups. The Professor and Kwame would teach them how to date the pieces and how to clean them. Later, an artist would be coming to draw the artefacts for further reference and a conservationist to begin restorative work. The day, therefore, would be spent in the lecture room, sorting, cleaning and learning.

"This is the boring part," Akete muttered to Monica who sat beside him.

"Like everything. There's always a boring part," she agreed.

"Who said this is boring?" Kwame asked. "This is the exciting part. This is all part of the discovery. This is where we establish the evidence."

"Evidence," Akete muttered. "Like a murder story, wid us as the police?"

"Something like that," Kwame said, but the rain came down again suddenly, and his words were lost in the noise.

The day proceeded with the students getting sleepier and sleepier, with frequent downpours coming to drown out their words. The local radio station reported a few landslides and some livestock being washed away.

As they worked, Kwame and the Professor helped them to sort and date the artefacts. They had found beads, pottery, pieces of clay pipes and even an old coin that the professor was particularly excited about. Most of the artefacts could be dated back to the late eighteenth and early nineteenth century. The Professor said that they would find earlier artefacts when they dug deeper.

They found factory-made pieces of pottery on the site of the great house, some probably originating from the best pottery houses in Europe. There were pieces with sophisticated painted patterns which still bore the signs of their former elegance. The pottery found on the slave site tended to be of rough earthenware with an occasional glazed piece.

Kwame explained that these were pots that the slaves had made themselves, in the manner of the Akan potters of West Africa. They were hand-cast, he told them, probably made by the women, they were in West Africa, and fired on an open fire rather than in a kiln. That was why they hadn't survived so well, to show the real beauty of their shaping. Such pots were still made in rural Jamaica and known as yabba pots. This was from a Twi word, the language of the Akans, *ayawa*, which meant vessel or dish.

"But the slaves had a little cash I guess," Akete said as he cleaned a piece of white glazed pottery with coloured designs on it. "This had some class."

"Remember they had their provision grounds and sold their goods in the Sunday market. Maybe they could buy something once in a while," Monica replied.

"Make pretend they free?' said Akete.

"Yes, can you imagine it, Akete? Not knowing anything about taking care of your own needs, even though you are a full grown man. Never making your own decisions. Not owning even yourself!" Monica sat back in her chair and thought for a long while.

"Then August first, 1833 and freedom. You out on the road

on your own. No land, no house, no job, nothing," said Akete.

"But your two long hands and freedom." Monica added.

"But what a gift! Freedom! The backra give you back what belongs to you. Yourself." Akete brushed a piece of dirt off the pottery he was cleaning.

Carla sat in the corner of the room and heard snatches of the conversation. She wished she could have heard more but the rain was pounding down on the corrugated iron roof again. There didn't seem much chance of talking to David that day, what with the Professor stalking the room like a hawk and the volume of painstaking work to be done.

Lunch time came and they had sandwiches with lemonade and fruit. Then they returned to work. Akete needed a spliff but restrained himself because he did not want to displease the Professor; the day dragged on and on for him. The Professor was cool, Carla was thoughtful, and David did his work with a kind of detachment that showed that he had his mind on other things.

The day drifted into dinnertime and evening. The rain slowed and the showers became fewer. The lights went on in the big room and then it was time for Kwame to take over and show the slides that had been promised them.

They all sat around the room with their eyes turned to the blank wall. The lights were put out and only the roar of the still angry sea and the distant sound of reggae music at some rum bar out on the main road disturbed the quiet. Kwame began to speak.

"I am going to show you a few slides of some villages in Ghana. These are traditional villages in which most of the old customs remain, in spite of some Western contact. The people cling to the old ways and the chiefs, sometimes, will not permit anything else. The buildings you will see here are wholly indigenous, as are the clothes. The cities, of course, show far more Western influence."

Akete leaned back in his chair. He no longer needed a spliff. This was food for his soul. He was now learning about the black continent from the words of a true inhabitant.

Kwame continued. "The African who is stripped of his values, his religion and his customs is confused. It is important for you to remember this. Most of you will have read Achebe's *Things Fall Apart* and having read it will understand the dilemma of many Africans today. Must he substitute the new for the old, and if he does, how will the assimilation of new cultures and customs affect the African way of life? At what price change? Are we part of a world dominated by capitalism and Western values or can we return to the past? At what price the retention of the old values of our ancestors?"

Kwame put the first slide in. It was the photograph of an African woman with a bundle of wood on her head, breasts bared, barefooted, tall and magnificent, looking like a queen.

Kwame looked at the group wondering how they would respond to a way of life that many in the Caribbean regarded as 'uncivilised'.

The second slide showed children standing beside a house, dome-shaped and as red as the mud that had made it. There was a small girl dressed in little else but copper anklets and a strip of cloth across her waist, with her hair low cut to her skull. She was beautiful. Akete had a rapt look on his face. Carla sat with her hands against her cheek in deep concentration. They listened intently while Kwame pointed out the various features of the scene in front of them.

Kwame then put in another slide. It was the interior of the house. He pointed to two beds, one was traditional, built into the ground, the other was a bed with a sprung mattress. Around the bed stood clay containers used for storing water and an aluminium pot for cooking. Above the bed hung a plastic portable wardrobe and there were some traditional clothes hanging from nails near the ceiling. A baby slept on the mattress. Kwame indicated that this kind of mixing of the traditional and the Western was typical of many villages nearer the urban centres.

It was when Kwame put in another slide showing an old dome-shaped structure outside a house that Martin was moved to ask, "What is that?"

"An oven," said Kwame. "It's built of stones and mud. In the dry season the bread is baked there, and in the wet season the chickens are put there to roost."

"They put chickens to roost in the same place they put the food?" Martin asked.

"But they don't do it at the same time. The ovens are carefully cleaned after the rainy season."

"Bread baked in chicken shit. Ugh!" Martin made a face.

Akete spoke. He had been silent for a long time. "Then where you was when Europe wallowed in mud? Where you was when people eat so much from rats that they died of the plague? Where you was when the towns and the cities did stink from garbage? Where you was when the baby was bathed in the same pot that they cooked the soup in? Where you is now that the British still bathe, if they bathe at all, in the kitchen sink? And how often *you* bathe, if you bathe at all?"

Akete was so angry that he spat the words out. Martin was pale. Kwame stood and watched the drama. He was perplexed and confused. Only the Professor remained calm. He spoke to quell the discord,

"This is a clash of stereotypes," he said icily. "There is a serious discussion to be had about the different cultural and historical frameworks that Akete and Martin speak from. But we can't have it if we descend to abuse and crude overstatements. Akete cut the crap. It's not necessary. We don't establish the legitimacy of our position on the basis of mocking the other. We all have to live on this planet. If we are to survive, we have to tolerate each other no matter how much we dislike each other's ways."

The Professor's voice was competing with the music coming from the rum bar. They were playing Peter Tosh. "Oh Rass Claat, O Bumbo claat".

The Professor continued, "In spite of the Man of Galilee, we still do not love our neighbour. In fact, some of us do not even love ourselves. We ridicule the very skin we wear. Life is full of complexities. Kwame, why don't you continue. Martin and Akete, cut the crap."

Akete looked at the Professor for a while, his eyes red with anger. The man should be defending him. He had a black skin and woolly hair. The man had suffered from Babylon just like himself.

There was silence in the room for a full minute, then Kwame continued. Each slide spoke for itself. Outside an owl hooted in a tree. The rain had gone with the passing of the day. The crickets murmured. Carla spoke softly to herself,

In the shadow of the night
the people fight
let the daylight come...

CHAPTER 8

The night was ink black by the time Akete went down to the beach for a swim. He walked carefully along the sand with his towel in his hands, his bare feet touching the ground lightly. He had seen a glimpse of the Africa he idealised. The huts and the stove were not new to him; he had seen them before in books, but the slides had brought them closer and he wanted to know more. He had to go there, to learn more about his homeland and feel the welcome that he was sure would come to him, to go there and swing his locks low and feel that he had, at last, come home.

Akete put the towel on the beach and dived into the water. He swam strongly. The waves moved under him as he swam. Now and again he went under the water, submerging his head deep, then surfacing for air. He went far out to sea, beyond where he could still feel the sand under his feet. He had been forced to learn to swim when he was a child; it that was one of the few things that he was glad his father had forced him to do. Now he really loved the sea.

The waters looked murky in the dark night, a deep blue flecked with black. He thought of the fish under him and felt a fleeting fear. In the darkness of the sea he was sure he could scarcely be seen, but he was no longer Ralph Ellison's invisible man. It frightened the white man. The black race was moving like a huge tidal wave towards their own shore.

He, Akete, had his skin, his learning and his pride. He was going to struggle and he was going to win. But there were times when he wondered if Africa would be as welcoming as he had thought it would be. To which tribe would he belong? How would he deal with the customs that he did not understand? Who were his African brothers? Would they see him as a brother? He had heard that West Indians were considered by some Africans as the children of slaves and therefore not of the same class as Africans. He knew, too, that many Jamaicans regarded Africans as less civilised than themselves – another result of the propaganda of the whites. Always the policy of divide and rule. If only there was unity among his race. He was glad that Kwame had come. Now he needed to go to Africa and to see for himself.

Akete swam on. His hands hit the water with force. He thought of the group at the hotel. The white boys. The Professor. The girls. In particular Carla. He had not yet spoken to her about the two men. He wondered how he would approach her about it. She looked so innocent. Untouched. He did not want her to be initiated into sex by one of those two who really only wanted some fun for a while. There was no future there. She needed someone of her own. Akete thought about his woman, Shadi, and their daughter. He loved those two. He wondered what he would do if Sheba faced the same problem when she was older. A surge of anger hit him. Carla was young and he wanted to protect her. Especially from that sneaky white bastard, David. If he tried to touch Carla, he would deal with him. Too many black women had been spoilt by the white masters. Akete lifted his face and spat out the salt water. Then he went down again under the surface.

Akete felt rather than heard the huge fish. He felt the movement of a barracuda, or was it a shark? What the hell should he do now? Where could he run? Run? Should he stay still or try to frighten off whatever it was? His mind went blank for a moment. He saw the barracuda move under him and he began to thrash about in the sea. Thank God it was not a shark. But even a barracuda could kill him. He had to scare it off. Beating the water might do that. Finding great reserves of energy, he swam and thrashed about, swam and hit the water with his hands and feet, up and down and around. That would at least confuse the fish.

For a brief moment, Akete thought about dying. Sheba, his child. Shadi, his woman. He had given her that name. Shadi. He felt the fish move closer under him, and he began again to splash about in the water. He looked up over the wave and saw the shoreline come closer and closer. He splashed and splashed again. The rhythm of his movements seemed to be doing its work. The fish, floundering a bit, seemed to be going away.

Akete hit out for the beach, still splashing furiously. It hindered his progress but he knew that he had to do it. His lungs were tightening in his chest and his heart was pounding as he drove himself towards the shore. The barracuda went away, confused. Akete stumbled through the shallows and flopped down on the warm sand. Hours seemed to have passed since he had left the shore, though he knew it was only minutes. Relief swept over him like a huge wave.

"Jesu Christos," he muttered under this breath. "That was close."

He lay on his back looking up at the stars. "Christ! What the hell me doing here?"

The stars looked like faraway worlds. Like the dream that Martin Luther King had wanted to reach. Like the heavens he often heard about and did not really believe in.

"What a world!" he said as he lay there on the sand. "What a great, huge, gigantic, turbulent world. Where me going to find peace in it? Where de great tranquillity? Why me so sad, so confused, so lonely? Dear God, so lonely? Why me fuss and fume so?"

The faraway stars seemed to reply. "We don't care," winking their lights in the darkness. "Who do you think you are, you lonely, confused man?"

The sea came in slowly and went out slowly again. Akete felt the rhythm and smiled. The stars were far away. They would not hurt him. He stood up and stretched. Then he went and found his clothes and started to walk back to the hotel, water dripping from his locks. His bare feet touched the sand, sinking into it, shifting the particles with his toes. When he reached the dry sand it clung to his feet.

For a moment Akete remembered his mother, the stern schoolteacher who had taught him what she termed the 'right values'. Then he thought of his father, the judge, absolute in his upholding of the law, who saw black as black and white as white, no shades, no delicate grey, no compromise.

When Akete left their household they had turned their backs on him and he knew that he could not return, not unless he cut off his locks, shaved the beard from his face and once more adopted the facade of respectability.

As he moved towards his quarters he thought about his family. Not his mother and father now, but his woman and his child. He loved those two. Christ! He really loved those two! And he had almost died. What if the barracuda had caught him? He had to live. He had his child, Sheba, to live for. But where did her future lie? What would she do with her life? What would she face? She would either join the fight or join Babylon. That was why he wished to burn down all the mighty citadels, all the almighty rites that had haunted his childhood. He wanted to cleanse the earth, remake the world with a new set of gods and a new reality. He had his learning and he had his pride but he knew he lacked the larger vision of Martin Luther King or Marcus Garvey, or the words of Marley and the intensity of Malcolm X. Well, he could still try to live his life in his own style.

Akete got into bed and slept in his bathing trunks.

When the sun woke him he wondered where he was for a moment. He heard the lap lap of the waves against the sand and everything came back – the terror of what had happened the night before. He shivered. Then he rolled out of bed and prayed for a moment to Jah. Life was sweet. He had faced the dreaded barracuda and won. He went to the bathroom and bathed. Then he slipped into his jeans and a cool T shirt. As he walked down the grass towards the kitchen he wondered what he would cook that morning. Cooking his own food, ital food, no salt, gave him a sense of being special, a little lion in his own den.

That morning he decided he would have an egg with callaloo cooked in coconut milk, and a cup of specially grated home chocolate, with the fat swimming on the top.

"Morning," he said to the cook as he marched into the kitchen. "Morning bredda," she replied. "How you do this morning?"

"All right," Akete said, smiling at her.

"Good. The others almost done eat. Why you so late"?

"Oversleep," he replied, as he began to fix his meal.

It was nearly half past eight when Akete came into the dining room with his food piled onto a plate. The Professor was still sitting there, reading the morning newspaper. He had a pencil in his mouth and was chewing on it like a man in deep thought.

"Oh Akete, there you are." he said. "I wanted to see you."

"Yes, Professor Milton?" said Akete.

"Yes. I want you and David and Carla to do a separate excavation near the slave village site. It was the slaves' burial site we think. We saw what looked like graves when we surveyed the plantation from the air."

"But," said Akete disturbed, "Professor, I don't know..."

"Don't worry. Kwame has agreed to oversee that site as well as the slave village site. I have already told Carla and David about it. You should enjoy it. We want to find out whether the slaves buried any funerary objects with their dead."

"But we might disturb someone's grave, one of our own black ancestors. Wouldn't that be disrespect?"

"The dead will hardly care, Akete. They'll be passing a story onto us that they couldn't tell. And we can still be respectful in the way we treat their remains."

Akete made a face.

"Bit pensive today, old man," said David as he glanced at Akete as they were loading the jeeps.

Akete looked up at him.

"I have me own thoughts," he said quietly.

"Well penny for them," said David. He wanted to be friends with this guy now that they would be working together.

"Save your pennies," said Akete. Then suddenly, he looked up at David and grinned. "I man fine," he said.

Encouraged by this gesture David continued. "So we'll be digging together now?"

"I know," said Akete. "The Prof told me."

"Well, what do you think?" asked David.

"Don't know yet, still thinking" said Akete.

"OK," David said and smiled shyly at him.

When they arrived at the estate, Kwame led his group to the new site and directed them to line it out before they began to excavate. It took the entire morning. David and Carla worked hard but Akete seemed tired and listless. Kwame wondered if having no salt in his diet contributed to Akete's tiredness, but he dared not mention it. Akete guarded his religion like a beloved woman.

Later that day, they began to find the first evidence of graves. Carla smiled at David as he whistled his way through a layer of stones and crude mortar.

"Do you think you've found some kind of tomb?" she asked.

"Possibly," he said. The thought of uncovering bones didn't really appeal to him.

"I wonder if the body will be a man's or a woman's?"

"You bet it's a man!" he said teasingly. "Only men would be given this kind of tomb."

"What do you mean?" she asked.

"Well he must have been some kind of chieftain in the slave village to get this kind of notice, don't you think?"

"Oh, I don't know. African peoples thought highly of their women. In some societies there were matriarchies where property was handed down from woman to woman. I'm sure women were equally honoured."

"But in a slave village?"

"Why not in a slave village?" asked Carla. "Even if they were forced into slavery, didn't mean these people lost their respect for each other." She squatted on the ground in her soiled jeans and looked up at David seriously. "And old people, whether men or women, were always thought of highly in African tribes. Not like in your country where they're dumped in old age homes and left to die."

"Oh, come on, Carla. We're not as bad as that!"

"That's what you think." Carla stood up and brushed off her jeans. "Anyway, I am sure it will be an old woman, the queen of the village," she added somewhat testily.

"Oh look! Look at this!" David shouted as he groped among the stones. "Look!"

"Oh really, David, it's only a grass snake. What are you doing with that thing?"

"It'll be the site mascot," he said as he stroked the long thin body.

At that moment, Akete came striding towards them. He had gone down to the jeep for a brief gossip with the drivers.

"Akete!" shouted David. "Look! A snake!"

"A snake? Man, put that reptile away. I and I man don't live with snakes. I and I man don't like reptiles."

"Ah, come on. It won't even bite. Touch him, Carla."

"No!" Carla said laughing. "No! I don't think so. And by the way, David, please wash your hands before you eat."

"Oh come on, for God's sake. It's just an innocent little grass snake. Still, if you think he's so bad, I'll name him Cain. Like in the Bible."

Akete looked scornful. "Site mascot, my ass," he muttered. "Why don't you kill the bloody thing or let me kill it for you."

David looped the snake over his arm as he found a plastic bag brought to put artefacts in. He punched a few holes in it and put the snake in. Then he rejoined his colleagues at work.

"These white people!" muttered Akete as he watched the proceedings. "Strangest creatures on the face of the earth."

David pretended not to hear and went back to his digging. He was a bit red when he looked up and grinned at Carla but he was happy now. He felt that at last he was beginning to break through her cool exterior and even establish some kind of relationship with Akete.

They worked on through the rest of the afternoon and well into the evening. Akete often looked at David. His skin was now quite red and almost beginning to peel. Akete's skin was darkening in the sun. Like the days of slavery, Akete thought to himself as he prised up a piece of mortar from the ground. Only then the black men were beaten and the white men were the beaters.

The more Akete thought about what they were doing, the more it disturbed him. Maybe just Carla and himself should be doing this job. They were breaking into a black man's tomb, a black man's secrets and he did not want to share any of that with David. It was sacrilege. Like moving into someone's bedroom during the wedding night.

Akete's frown deepened. He needed a spliff, though maybe a cigarette would do.

David saw Akete pause and wipe his hand across his forehead.

"Tired?" he asked him.

"I need to cool mi brain," Akete replied. "Sun still hot as hell."

"Need a cigarette?" David straightened up and pulled a cigarette from the pack of ten he had in his pocket.

Akete nodded.

"Let's both take a draw," David said as he lit Akete's cigarette and moved towards a large stone under the star-apple tree. Akete moved towards another stone and sat down. He drew the smoke deep into his nostrils and exhaled slowly. Carla straightened up from the backbreaking task and joined them. David grinned at her.

"Want a smoke too?"

"No thanks. Just water I need. You know I don't smoke."

"I know, little angels don't smoke do they?"

Carla smiled at him. She did not see Akete scowl. She poured water from the igloo into a plastic cup and sat on the grass. She sipped slowly, as though she was drinking wine.

CHAPTER 9

Carla sat up in bed that night and thought about her mother. She supposed that she did love her but she still remembered the years when she'd had to fight to gain her independence and grow into a real person who could stand up to her mother's strong will. It had been a struggle even to leave home for the university campus. Her mother wanted her to study but she felt sure she would lose her daughter. She'd had to fight against this overprotectiveness all her life. Although she wasn't chaperoned to go to church functions she couldn't go to a movie in the town alone. Then, after she'd left home and gone to university, her mother's nagging had taken another tone. Had she found a man yet? When was she going to settle down? What about grandchildren? How could she do that without a husband? She hoped Carla would not come home after studying with a baby and no father. What would the neighbours say? And then she had extended that nagging to the question of race. Were there any fair-skinned men in her group? Did she like them? Did they like her? And although she did not say it, Carla knew that a very dark-skinned man as a husband would not meet with her mother's approval.

It was not that her father was a weak man, but he preferred to keep in the background. Looking back now Carla saw that his strength lay in his quiet wisdom. She loved her father dearly and felt now that he had sat back because he knew that he could not fight her battles for her, that he had to let her fight them for herself. She was now a stronger person with a real knowledge of what she wanted. Moreover, in spite of her mother's resentment at her new found independence, Carla knew that she had gained her mother's respect.

But she still remembered with pain the many years of being forced into submission. The weapon her mother used was not the force of the whip, but the even greater force of weeping and wailing.

"Look at what I do for you," she would say between her tears. "You are an ungrateful wretch. You cyan do without you mother and you father. What you think I send you to Sunday school for? The Bible say, respect you mother and you father that your days may be long." Then the tears would flow again. "Mi bring mi daughter into this world and she want to leave me so early. Is ungrateful, you ungrateful chile. Lord Jesus, take the case. Take the case, Lord Jesus. The good Lord see and know say I try. I try to raise you in the right and proper way."

Carla had once thought her father the henpecked victim of her mother's outbursts, but she knew now that he resisted through his silence. Her mother feared that silence and would have preferred a man with a loud voice who would fight openly and who, in the end, she would have been able to control. But her mother could not fight her father's silence and to this day she remained puzzled by it.

Carla flicked through the book on the bed beside her but what came into her thoughts were memories of her uncle, the young Uncle Joe, who had invaded her life when she was fourteen and left her shattered and full of hatred for him and distrust for men.

Uncle Joe had lived abroad all his life and had come back embittered by his experiences. He had been a soldier and a garbage man and had worked at just about any casual job he could pick up. He had tried to be a student and gain qualifications but had not succeeded at anything. All he ever did successfully was to lure women to his bed. He had no idea how many children he had fathered. Then he burst in upon her life and threatened to take her innocence away.

It had happened one Sunday afternoon. Carla and her uncle had been left alone in the house, the others having gone to a church function. She said that she needed to study and he said that he needed to rest. How naive she had been when he came into her room. How silly she had been when she had looked at some *Playboy* magazines he had brought with him and for the first time in her life had seen nude women in seductive poses. And why had she felt excited when he touched her breasts and offered to take her photograph in the nude? But she had been perplexed and hurt when he tried to force her to bed with him and she'd had to fight and beg him to leave her alone, knowing that it would have been a disaster both for her and for him. She had never told her parents. Uncle Joe had left two days later and she had never seen him again. But she still remembered and still despised him and had remained wary of all men ever since.

Carla thought about the discovery of the grass snake and David's friendliness. Would David behave like her Uncle Joe? She was a big woman now and shouldn't assume that all men were alike, but it was hard, very hard to forget what had happened. Maybe she could try though, maybe she could form a meaningful relationship with David, even if it only for a short time. But she wanted to make one thing absolutely clear: he had to respect her. She thought of Akete and his scorn for David. He was impetuous and fiery tempered, a fireball who would burn himself out sooner or later. She wondered about his protectiveness towards her, as though there were some danger around her, something that he wished to help her to avoid. He couldn't really think she was in any real danger from either David or the Professor. And she thought again, if Akete was a free man without a woman and a child, could she or would she want to take him home to her parents?

The answer to the first was a resounding no. She could almost see her father quietly pitching him out of the house, not with physical force but with the force of the word. She could hear her mother weeping: "I tell you, I bring up the chile to respect Jesus Christ and she going roun' wid rasta man. Lord help me and mi distress at this time. Lord help me head and mi pressure. Mi daughter going to kill me off before mi time." Carla sighed. There was so much complexity in the world, so many taboos.

It was not until late that night that she slept. She awoke next morning to a bright sun and a bad headache. That headache always came when she had not slept well and it usually bothered her for the rest of the day. She took an aspirin and bathed, put on a pair of jeans and a clean cotton blouse and went downstairs. Breakfast was almost finished.

The Professor looked at her. "Carla," he said pointedly, "you're very late this morning."

"I am sorry, Professor. I overslept."

"Carla overslept, an unusual occurrence for such a dedicated young archaeologist. Don't you agree with me, Carla?"

Carla kept her eyes down to hide her fury. She was angry. The headache was not making things any better. Blast it, if only she could walk out of this place and never come back! But calm prevailed as she counted slowly to ten. She ignored the Professor and ate her meal. She hoped that no one noticed her shaking hands and the wobble that came to her legs as she stood up to leave the table.

When Sonia smiled at her as they went to the jeep together Carla felt better. Also the aspirin had begun to work.

"Don't worry, Carla," said Sonia. "The Prof is in a rotten mood today. Just stay away from him. That's all."

Carla nodded. "It wouldn't be so bad if I didn't have this terrible headache. I didn't sleep too well last night."

"Why?" Sonia asked her.

Carla shrugged her shoulders. "Don't know. Just one of those nights, I suppose."

The birds were at it again in the trees about the hotel compound and Carla felt lightened as she looked up at them. The sun cast a bright light over everything, reminding her of August mornings at home in the hills of Manchester. The air was always so clean there and the large white clouds that sometimes came looked like freshly washed bed sheets against the blue. If the sun shone through them there were yellow glints of light at their edges, like a sharpened sword against firelight.

Carla loved her home. Often the blue sky flecked with white seemed like a canopy over her own particular Eden. When it rained or when it was windy and cool, as it so often was, or when the Christmas breeze came up from the sea in late November and the hogberry trees were full of fruit and the bitter bush was in bloom and the wild rosemary smelled sweet and clean in the scrubby grass of the cow pasture, Carla thought that her home was perfect.

She remembered the songs of the birds in the trees, the tiny grass quits that came to feed on grass seeds, the ominous black birds that sometimes warned of sickness, the white headed bald pate and yellow canary, the banana bird and the chicken hawks. She remembered too the swift running mongooses and the fights between the mongooses and the dogs. Carla loved the mongooses, the dapper look they wore as they stood still for a while and looked at you. They made her think of dressed-up Englishmen in tails stepping out to dinner.

But she came back to the task of the day and helped to load the jeep. They were all moving at a slow pace that morning.

At the grave site, David came over the hill towards her with his gloves in one hand and a shovel in the other. He grinned.

"Well Carla, how goes it?" he asked.

"Oh, I'm all right," she replied as she bent down to her task.

"Oh come on Carla, chat with me a while. You're such a pretty girl."

"David, leave me alone."

"I wish I could get to know you better."

"David, leave me."

David moved closer to her, reached out his hand and gently stroked her hair. Carla removed his hand from her head.

"David, be careful."

"Come on, how about a kiss? Just a teeny weeny little peck."

"David, please."

"Okay, maam."

And he bent and kissed her on the cheek.

At that moment Akete came striding down the hillside to see David carefully put a lock of hair back in place on Carla's forehead. He was going to deal with that white boy.

Seeing Akete approach, both David and Carla began to dig away at the grave. They looked confused. David's face was flushed and Carla refused to look up from her task. Akete took up a shovel and began to dig away mercilessly at remaining mortar covering the grave. Before long they had reached the softer earth underneath it.

They were digging up the secrets of someone's life, Akete thought. Digging, digging, digging away at someone's life and secrets and private feelings, digging away at a poor dead man's life and he not even knowing it. Or did he? Did the dead know the secrets of the living?

After a while Akete called Carla aside. David looked at them but kept on digging at the earth and stones.

Akete plunged his penknife into a knot of stiff grass and said to Carla from his seat on a stone, some distance away from the grave, "The I man a watch dem two man deh. Careful. No future wid the old one, no future wid the white one. Careful, daughter. I an I man see what happen a while back. Man is man. Some want woman to settle with. Some want woman to use. Just remember that. I an' I just a tell you. Just in case you fall. An' you is a nice daughter. Got you life ahead of you and you future full. All right? Take care."

Carla watched closely as Akete took the knife from the grass root and wiped it against his pants. The red dirt stained the pants but Akete did not seem to care. Carla noted the look in his eyes. It was a look that she had often seen in her father's eyes. Protectiveness. Gentleness, almost love, the love of a man for his daughter.

Carla smiled at him. She felt her eyes fill with tears. She did not know why, but she suddenly cared so much for Akete, as a good friend. She knew that he would defend her as fiercely as he would defend anyone of his race, particularly a woman. There was a gentleness about him that appealed to her. He was complex, not just thunder, but also gentle rain. Quietly she reached out to touch his hand, "Akete, thanks," she said, and wondered why a flood of relief swept over her. Someone cared. Someone wanted the best for her. And he was a man. Not all men were like Uncle Joe.

"All right, daughter." He smiled at her, walked back to the grave site and bent to help David. Carla joined them after a few minutes. Methodically they chipped away at the earth.

Kwame came and watched them now and again and then left them to it. This was routine work and they did not need him yet, not till any bones began to show. The sun beat down on their backs and on their unprotected heads and David thought of home. It would still be quite cool there even if the sun was shining. He kept his head down and so did Carla. Akete stopped for a while and moved to rest under a tamarind tree. They saw him take a drink of water and lie backwards on the grass.

Neither of them noticed Akete leave the site. They were both too busy digging, heads down and hard at work.

It was towards evening that David was reminded of his new pet, the grass snake.

"How is Cain?" Carla asked, just as the setting sun was signalling the end of another day's work.

"Cain is all right. I left him in my room."

Kwame came to make a last check. "Now let's see," he said stroking his tiny goatee beard. "You've got down to about level four on this site. Nice work. Any finds worth noting?"

"No, just a few pieces of china among the mortar and the stones."

"I hope you labelled them and put them away."

"Oh yes. Carla did all of that!"

"Where is Akete?"

"In the back somewhere... I don't know."

"Doing what?"

"I guess he's having a smoke or so," said David.

"I'll have to see about that," Kwame said as he gathered in the plastic bags of artefacts.

They took the gear and walked down the hill towards the jeeps. All the others were there, except Akete.

"Let's wait a few minutes for him," said the Professor as he looked at his watch.

They stood and waited for ten minutes, then the Professor said, "OK. Akete knows his way back and I'm hungry. So let's go, shall we?"

A few minutes later the jeeps were roaring over the bumpy track and then the paved roadway. No one saw Akete appear over the hill and wave at them frantically. All were too busy thinking about eating and the lecture that Kwame would give that night. Although the dig was absorbing and the artefacts of great interest, they were getting tired now. They all went to their rooms for a rest until the bell ring for supper.

Akete had still not arrived when they went to the lecture room, but no one was really worried. He seemed to know his way about the place. As Martin remarked to David, "No one knows the ins and outs of this country like a rastaman. I bet he goes to the ends of this country to cultivate or buy his weed. Back to the little African." They walked up the steps. "Wonder what he'll come with today? More chicken roosts? Or goats pens?"

"Oh come on," David said as they went through the door, "I don't think you're being fair. I thought that what he had to say about African culture was really interesting."

"What about those poor half-dead people you see on the TV news? They have a rich culture?" Martin said. "How can he pretend that Africa can sustain itself. Are they the ones who deal with the results of the famines brought on by their inefficient farming methods and their wars? Oh, no, when that happens who else stops them from starving but the Western aid agencies and Western governments. But where's that recognition in Kwame's little talks? No, I don't see much civilisation in those mud huts."

David frowned. "What is civilisation though? How can we say we are more civilised than anyone else? By what criteria do we judge civilisation?"

"David, don't tell me you are beginning to swallow that nonsense. Please, don't tell me that." Martin's voice held a kind of mock pain.

"It's nothing like that," David replied. "It's just that I think we've got to be fair. They have their own kind of life. We have ours. We have to respect them too."

Martin responded with a deep grunt. He muttered something under his breath about not confusing civilisation with wanting to get inside a little black girl's panties. David did not hear what he said and there was no time for the conversation to continue as the rest of the group had joined them in the room.

"No Akete yet?" asked the Professor.

"No sir," Martin answered, "not yet!"

"OK. We can't wait on him. Let's start as soon as we're all settled. Akete is not a child."

Kwame began to tell them about the traditional way of building African houses, the skills in the use of local materials to suit the climatic conditions: the use of thatch or similar materials for roofing, mud for the walls, the coolness of the interiors, the use of mud tablets for the traditional beds in the houses, of the monkey jars to keep the water cool and the food healthy and clean, and that African pottery was at last getting international recognition for its beauty. He told them about the adaptation of the West African house to the Caribbean environment during the period of slavery.

He told them of the African way of laying out the village, and the important role of the African chief and his family. He spoke of the many traditional customs that had held Africans together as a people, that whilst there were different tribal customs, there was much that was common to all West African peoples. He explained how many of these customs had come to the Caribbean and had survived in some form through slavery, despite the conscious attempts of the plantation managers to suppress any aspects of African culture that might encourage resistance.

He told them too how the villages had been linked into states with impressive cities such as Benin and how the whole of Africa had been connected by trade routes and long-established patterns of trade with India and the Middle East.

David listened with a growing sense of how little he really understood about African culture and its survivals in the Caribbean, and even Martin was moved to silent interest.

Monica was the first to question Kwame when he had finished speaking.

"How did people get around before the introduction of cars and trains and trucks and buses? What beast of burden did Africans use?"

"In the North there was always the camel. Elsewhere there was the donkey. In West Africa during the time of the great empires of Mali, Songhai and earlier, Old Ghana, salt and gold were carried by donkeys."

"These empires you mention, how important were they? Were they as extensive as say Rome was in its time?" asked David.

"They were extensive, though not to the same extent as Rome. But these empires lasted a long time, over a thousand years, and their influence spread over vast areas of the continent. Even into Egypt and parts of Arabia. To Europe too, particularly Spain. The Arabs who crossed the Sahara and traded in West Africa introduced many African goods to Europe, goods like cotton cloth, pottery and carving."

"Egypt," Kwame added, "contrary to popular opinion was a black civilisation. Yes. The pyramids are our creation. The people of Egypt were mainly black people during the time of the some of the pharaohs. Kushites from the south, black people, ruled Egypt for a long period." He reflected for a moment. "Pity Akete is not here. I wanted to have him in on this lecture. He would have a lot to say on this. He told me he'd read a great deal about ancient Africa."

"What about medicine?" Martin asked after a pause in the conversation. "Are witch doctors, or were witch doctors for real? Could they really cure?"

"Witch doctors, or tribal healers as they are sometimes called, still cure people. These people know about roots and herbs, and their effects on the human body, even if they don't know much about the chemicals in the herbs. In fact," Kwame added, "many European doctors, especially those on the continent, are anxious to get back to using herbs and the roots. They are at last recognising their true value."

"What about the oral tradition?" the Professor asked. "We still have some of that element here among black people."

"Very, very important. The histories of the tribes are in the heads of the griots, not always on the written page. Africans taught in more traditional style at the University of Timbuktu, but essentially it is the griot who carries the history of the tribe."

"A great resource then," said David, "to students of African history."

"Still a great resource," Kwame agreed. "We've got to capture the knowledge in the heads of the old griots before they go with it to their graves."

They were full of questions and at last Carla felt they were coming together. They would still disagree and still look at things in different ways, but that was good because without it there would be boring consensus, but now they were listening to each other with respect. Pity Akete was not there. Where was he?

The session continued late into the night.

"Thanks, Kwame," the Professor grunted as he eventually stood to dismiss the gathering. "I think you have cleared up a few misconceptions about the continent of Africa. Don't you agree, Martin?"

"Yes Prof, this has made me think a great deal."

"Yes," David said. "I am doing that too."

Outside, the stark blackness of the night was broken by the staccato lights of stars in the sky, and, like stars themselves, the peenie wallies, tiny moving pinpoints of light, flew everywhere. A screech owl sounded in a tree nearby. Carla shivered, although the night was warm.

CHAPTER 10

Akete sat up and rubbed his eyes. He looked around him. He was feeling chilly and confused. Where was everybody and what was he doing sleeping on the ground like this? He remembered that he had wandered off to have a smoke. The ganja had been potent and good and it had calmed his agitation. Then he had slept. His head hurt as he tried to stand, then he had stumbled to his feet and walked over the hill and seen that both David and Carla had gone. He had seen the jeep set off up the road and he had shouted and waved but no one appeared to have seen him.

As the effects of the weed began to wear off, he felt low. He needed another draw or at least a good night's sleep. Raas! Why had the others left him behind? Blasted middle-class baldheads! He wanted his home in the ghetto with his cornmeal porridge and his chicken neck and back and his callaloo cooked to perfection by his woman. He wanted to join in a drum session with his fellow Rastafarians. He wanted his woman and child and suddenly, unexpectedly, he missed his mother.

He remembered David's attentions to Carla and he felt even more angry than he had at the time. Carla was a black woman and a black woman untouched. No white man was to have her, especially if it was the first time. He knew that

David was just fooling around and had no good intentions towards the girl. Slavery had seen enough of the exploitation of black women; he would deal with the white boy if he made another move.

He decided to go to a Rastafarian yard he knew was a few miles away from the hotel. They sold curios to tourists and weed and natural juices to passing motorists. He had enquired about them from the hotel manager and learned that they were a hard working group who were rarely in trouble with the police. In fact, the manager said, some policemen actually went there now and again for drumming sessions. There were rumours, though, that someone in the group had begun to deal in crack cocaine. Akete was to be careful.

It was dark when Akete reached a large red yard on the other side of the village and joined the group of rastamen who sat there smoking and talking. The yard was on a hillside and secluded from prying eyes by a circle of trees and shrubs. Akete had been told of this yard by members of his own group in Kingston and had long wanted to visit it. Strange tales had been told about the leader of this group. Some said he was an obeah man, some a balmyard man, some a true messenger sent from Jah to deliver his people from downpression and lead them back to the kingdom of Jah Rastafari.

Akete felt good as he smelled the smoke and saw the red, gold and green flag flapping on a pole in the middle of the yard. He had come home.

For a time no one addressed him, then a young man with his locks tied in a red head-tie came forward. "Welcome breddaman."

Akete looked at him and smiled. "Thank yuh," he said. "Respec' due."

"Respect," others called from the sitting circle, their faces solemn in the evening light.

"Where de bredda coming from?" one man asked.

"The I man is from town," said Akete.

"And where in town is the man coming from?" asked another.

"Trench Town."

"Does the man know Ras Bolton, the leader of the tribe in that place?"

"The I man know Ras Bolton. The I man is a friend of Ras Bolton."

"Then the man is welcome," said an old man with matted locks almost falling to his waist. "The man is very welcome."

Handshakes and names were exchanged and a feast of goat and ital rice and peanut punch began when women appeared suddenly from the outdoor kitchen with food to serve to the men. Akete thought of his woman and smiled.

After the food, the chalice was passed around and Akete filled his nostrils and inhaled the smoke. It moved him so much that he felt that he could dance and dance. He needed his woman, he needed to hear the drum and he needed to fight Babylon.

The chalice went around again and the drumming began. Akete felt love and hate and desire and passion and bliss move through his soul with the swiftness of a flood. The drums kept moving him, pulling him in one direction and then the next. When the chanting began, Akete wanted to beat down Babylon, rid the world of its filth and the downpression that had plagued his people for so long.

Life was sweet and life was terrible and the elation gave way to depression and back to elation and to lightness and happiness and bliss and hope; but the fear crept back, and Akete was not free of hatred as the drums burst in upon his head. His greatest wish now was to destroy, to pull the evil away from the world that was once bliss but which had fallen into bad times because of the white man. Akete took another pull at the chalice and he felt sweeter than beet juice mixed with condensed milk, sweeter than peanut punch, sweeter than hard liquor when it hit the head, sweeter than sugar cane juice, sweeter than honey fresh from the hive. But as soon as the sweetness left him, the hate burned and he went to lie down, but got up again to take a draw as the chalice went around for the fourth time.

He wandered into one of the houses and a young man who was sitting there looked at him and said quietly, "The man want something stronger."

He handed him the white rock. It was the first time that Akete had used crack and he could not believe the purity of the fire that opened his veins and soared in his head. Then he fell to a depth he had never known before. Eventually, he went to sleep, but his sleep was uneven and troubled. When he woke he knew he had to kill Babylon before it destroyed him.

CHAPTER 11

Kwame looked over his notes for the next day's lecture, but somehow he could not concentrate. The world seemed upside down. The crickets outside sounded loud and unnatural. He could hear a screech-owl and he remembered his mother telling him that it was a harbinger of death or destruction. His thoughts strayed to the Professor. He still admired his knowledge and scholarship, but there was a lot that was petty about him, like his treatment of Carla for instance. He was obsessed with the girl. She was his student, not his mistress.

His thoughts moved to Martin and David. In a way these white boys were innocents. Brought up in white middle-class American homes in the suburbs and taught to think American white boy thoughts, they were both as narrow and as innocent as young crows. David, at least, seemed to be learning something from his experiences in Jamaica.

Kwame had lived in America long enough to hate some things and to admire others. What he really loved was the strength and resilience of the African Americans. True, there were some who had been crushed by their plight, but theirs had been an even harsher history than that of the people of the islands.

But the night was passing. Kwame needed to sleep. He thought of his mother's lullabies and his father's gentle touch.

He thought of his own children who had worked hard and bought him a bicycle to help him do his job as an archaeologist in those remote country districts where roads were often impassable by motor vehicles. He missed his wife's cooking, missed their moments in bed, missed her caring for him. He missed his land and his people and even though this land had many similarities to Ghana, not least in its people, it was still not home.

"Where the hell is Akete? That young man crazy or something?" the Professor said.

Martin grinned and muttered under his breath to David, who was busy putting gear into the jeep, "Rasta man gone walkabout. Clearing his head a bit, or maybe he's gone to his woman; the spliff made him feel for it."

David did not reply, and placed the grass snake in its little plastic bag carefully on the floor of the jeep.

Soon they were on its way to the plantation. The trees and grass were still full of the dew-water of the night and the singing birds crossed their way, to and fro, to and fro. Carla felt tense in spite of the morning's beauty as she thought about the day's task.

Today they would probably unearth the skeleton in the grave, if there was one. But Akete was not around and she and David would have to do it alone. She hoped that Kwame would help them, at least to get over the difficult parts, certainly when they finally had to take up the skeleton.

The Professor rode in the same jeep as Carla and she thought that she detected a tenseness in him too, no doubt over Akete, a bewilderment, as if he were working out a puzzle. David and Martin were the only jovial people in the group. They chatted and laughed and waved at passers-by, and cheered when a mongoose dashed halfway across the road, turned back in fear for its life and disappeared into the undergrowth.

When they arrived at the site, Carla put her water bottle under the shade of a tree. Then she and David, with Kwame occasionally helping, began to dig. Few words passed between them.

Slowly the stones and the mortar disappeared as the pit got deeper. The sweat poured out in bushels from their skins. As Kwame watched them digging side by side he could not miss the irony: one the child of the masters, the other the child of slaves.

The companionship between them grew. They grinned at each other over the dirt and stones. David knew that he had to give Carla space, that he could not just play with her feelings. They both sensed that a true friendship was growing.

When they came upon the first piece of bone, they felt a rush of anxiety, not of ghosts but over the task at hand. They must be careful now. This work was serious. They must photograph whatever they revealed before dislodging it. David went to call Kwame to help them.

Slowly the skeleton appeared. They dug carefully around it. The ribs, then the pelvis, then the bones of the legs. David took photos, Carla took photos and then they dug gently underneath the bones, the excitement growing on them as they progressed. Around the bones lay the remains of what had been a coffin. So this slave had been given a proper burial. He had not just been tossed into the grave without thought. However the masters treated the slaves, their own people ensured that they were buried with decency. Who had the man been? Kwame assured them that the bones were those of a man. Maybe he had held a good position on the estate, a head carpenter or a boilerman or maybe a driver, or even, who knows, the chief obeahman. Maybe he had been one of the thousands of field slaves whose lives had passed unremarked on Plantation Plains. Carla shivered. David looked up at her and grinned. He was enjoying himself.

Then they uncovered the skull. To Carla it appeared to lie there like a private diary exposed to prying eyes, a diary whose code could not be read. "It's wrong," she thought as she took a photograph of the skull. "It's absolutely wrong. How dare we disturb this man's rest, his sacred tomb? What right have we to play God with his past life?" She hated this moment. The black man's skull embedded in its mould of earth was the final exposure, the invasion of his innermost thoughts, his private dreams.

They continued digging until the entire skeleton could be seen. But it was not entire. One of the feet was missing.

"So what is this?" Kwame said as he watched the dirt being carefully removed from the area around where the foot should have been. "Do you realise what has happened here?"

"Oh God!" Carla said. "This man was a runaway."

"Why do you say that?" David asked.

"Because the usual punishment for a runaway was to have a foot amputated. Probably it was tossed to the dogs."

David went pale under his tan and shivered in the hot sun. "This is terrible," he said. "I've read about slavery, always thought of it as something dreadful, but in the past. This really brings it home... I don't know what to say..."

"Let's just remember this man's life. We don't know anything else about him," Carla said, "but we do know that he never accepted being a slave, that he had the courage to strike out for his freedom. Let's give him the respect he deserves. It's the least we can do."

They stood silently around the man's bones. The sun had gone behind a sudden cloud as if to shield him from its rays. The moment was tense as each of them thought their own thoughts. Each, though, felt they had made a discovery through this intrusion, after which nothing would ever be the same.

No one saw Akete come from behind the green thicket of bush from which the midget grassquits rose and took to the treetops in alarm.

"What the fuck are you doing?" Kwame screamed as Akete leapt into the grave. "Akete, what madness is this?"

Akete seemed neither to have seen or heard Kwame.

The rachet-knife in his pocket appeared and flew open in his hand. The blade sunk deep into David's stomach. Akete twisted. The blood seeped into the grave, onto the bones lying there. David fell on top of them.

He could see the deep blue of sky looming at him, saw the sun like a fire, saw the colours of the rainbow, the whiteness of the cloud, and knew that there was colour in everything, in the trees and the flowers, in the animals everywhere. He knew that he was a man like all the rest, no god, no ape, no tree. Then he saw nothing. The pain cut his gut and the warm blood washed his skin.

"Dear God, help me, help me please!" he cried.

Carla screamed.

Akete stood for a moment in the grave, then scrambled out of it, his face twisted in hate and anger. Then he seemed to realise what he had done and fled.

Kwame began to mutter as he gently tried to lift David from the grave. Carla's clothes were soaked with blood as she helped him. Why? Why?

She did not scream again, but her first scream had been heard and the scamper of feet and the shouts from the others as they came running added to the confusion.

When they lifted David to the embankment he was breathing slowly. A little cry escaped his lips. His face was twisted in pain and his eyes shone with fear. His voice came hoarse and choked from his throat.

"God help me, help me please!" he said again. Carla prayed silently that he must not die, could not die.

CHAPTER 12

Two days later, two days of hell and anxiety and the fury that raged in his head over the destruction of this project, the Professor was sitting in his hotel room. His head was in his hands. His hands propped on his knees. For this to happen! On the first project in his own country, just nearing the end of an illustrious career. Despair. The deepest kind of despair from a man who knew that he had aged greatly in two days, that his vitality, all that made him what he was, had gone like water into the clouds. These clouds hung about his head tormenting him, terrifying him.

It had been on the news, he had hit the headlines for the first time in his life and in the worst possible way. He had failed to control a situation that might have been averted, that might have been prevented had he been more alert to the warning signs in Akete's outbursts of anger, had he been firmer, more tactfully insistent in dealing with him. He saw no harm in a little relaxed smoking of weed, but that was not how the authorities would see it. They would see his failure to stop Akete smoking ganja whilst he was on the project as leading to the narcotic state in which he had evidently been when he tried to murder David.

Bile rose in his mouth. Angrily he swatted at a fly that hovered about his face. Had he been younger he would have had time to live this down. But doubtless he would now be going into forced retirement. He would be relegated to the position of reading the Bible at night, praying for his soul and kissing his equally ageing wife good night on the cheek. As he sat thus in the valley of the shadow of death, he thought of Akete for a while. Why had a promising young man like that allowed his mind to be taken over by drugs? Akete was an angry young man, but well intentioned. He had been an angry young man too. For him what had been important were books and the knowledge that he gained from them. The experience that came with learning had helped him through his anger, given him a deeper perspective on life. He had sometimes smoked a little weed in private, but had never allowed it to dominate his life.

But at least David had not died. Although still critically ill, the doctors anticipated a full recovery. Except for some possible problems with his stomach in the future, David would be fine.

He heard a tentative knock on the door and rose to answer it. He turned the key in the lock, twisted the doorknob and inched the door open. Before him stood Akete, dirty and dishevelled. His face looked grey and dead except that his eyes moved in their sockets. The eyeballs were red, as though coated with dust. Looking closer Professor Milton saw that there was penitence on his face. A look of deep sorrow. The sorrow of a man who had seen the fire of Lucifer and had come back to tell the tale.

"Prof," he muttered, his voice deep in his gut. "Prof."

Then anger spurted from the Professor's mouth, his spittle splashing Akete's face like spray from the sea.

"How dare you, how dare you come back here like this?"

Akete's body moved slowly, the body of a man in subjection, knowing his crime, appreciating his adversity.

"Prof, I want you to help me."

The Professor smiled. His voice was silky-sweet, soothing when it came. "OK, Akete," he said. "Come in, come in."

Akete moved into the room, relief etched on every sinew of his body, his thin face alight with hope. He knew that the Professor could not fail him.

As he opened the door and let Akete in, the Professor moved slowly, quietly outside.

"Just a moment," he said, "I'll soon be back."

He closed the door behind him and locked it. He went downstairs to the phone booth and dialled 119.

After the police cars had left the compound, Carla rose from her seat in the dining room and began to walk slowly down to the sea. She hoped that the lap lap of the waves would lull her, bring her peace. She wanted the breeze that came up from the sea to move gently across her face. She wanted to feel the slippery sand moving under her feet.

Carla wondered why she did not, as her mother would have done, turn to the Bible for comfort. She had not prayed since the moment after the attack. She felt that she could never pray again. God seemed too far away, too distant, too remote.

Kwame had helped the policemen take the submissive Akete from the Professor's room. Kwame had looked broken too, like a father who had lost a child. The police had expected a struggle; they came prepared with M16 rifles and batons. But Akete had hung his head on his chest and gone to them meekly. He had muttered as he entered the car.

"Sheba… Sheba…"

Kwame hoped that this was not the end for Akete. Perhaps he would serve time for the wounding and be sent to a detoxification unit. He had a good mind. He was valuable. He had done something terrible but his people needed him.

Martin had seen Akete as he moved handcuffed into the police jeep. He stood at the window and watched, his eyes red with anger.

"Bloody fool!" His hands had tightened on the windowsill. Then slowly he let go.

Monica and Sonia had stood outside watching Akete go. Perhaps after serving his punishment his anger would be tempered, become more focused, less violent. Sonia hoped that he would not be expelled from the university but be allowed to finish his studies after his sentence. They too both hoped that it would not be the end for him.

As she stood on the seashore, Carla reflected that she had regarded places like this, and her home on the South coast as little Edens, havens of peace and contentment. They were still places of great beauty, but she realised that she had always seen her land through comfortable and protected eyes. David had once asked her to tell him about her country, but she never had. She could have told him of the laughter of the people, the singing of the children and the beauty of the land, and he would have seen it that way. There was still truth in that, but now she could not see it with the same innocence.

There was to be an investigation. All were required to remain at the hotel until a team of investigators came down from the University. Then they would return to their own little worlds.

For a moment, if only for a brief moment, with David she had started to shed the cocoon that had held her safe. She knew she was vulnerable, still naive and vulnerable. But she no longer felt trapped in the fears of her childhood. She had begun to break free of the shell that bound her; it was time to test her wings. She would probably never see David again. She guessed that his feelings for her had never been particularly serious and that there were differences between them that would probably have made a relationship impossible, but there had been brief moments between them when they had shared something she would not forget.

Carla stood and looked at the sea. There were sharks and barracudas out there waiting to eat the unwary. On the land there were barracudas too: drug addicts, rapists, criminals – and old lechers. She thought of the Professor and her irritation with his unwanted attentions. She had once seen him as a little god, well, a very minor one. She was over that now.

She turned her back on the sea and moved inland. This scrubby land of hers had a strange beauty in spite of all its violence. A slight breeze lifted her dress above her knees. Uncaring, Carla walked across the white sand beach to her own room.

REDEMPTION SONGS:
BLACK HISTORY IN FICTION & POETRY FROM PEEPAL TREE PRESS

THE VIEW FROM BELMONT
Kevyn Alan Arthur

The View from Belmont tells two stories: one through the letters of a young English widow who takes over her husband's cocoa estate in Trinidad in 1823; the other through the responses of a group of contemporary Trinidadians.

Clara's letters present the insights of a perceptive, independent-minded and generous-spirited young woman, who is nevertheless wholly committed to the institution of slavery. The letters give a sharp sense of the wider Trinidadian society, but at their heart is an account of Clara's relationships with those with whom she shares her life on the estate, particularly Kano, a 'loyal' slave whom she takes to her bed.

For the contemporary Trinidadians, the letters raise troubling questions about the nature of the national psyche, the absence of social consensus and the extent to which the history that the letters describe still shapes the present. This is a comic, painful and moving novel. Its presentation of the cruelties, violence and the casual affections of everyday relations under slavery raise questions not only about the nature of Caribbean societies, but the nature of history and its interpretation.

Kevyn Alan Arthur is the author of a poetry collection, *England and Nowhere*, published by Peepal Tree in 1992.

ISBN: 1-900715-02-3
Pages: 230pp
Price: £7.99 $14.00 US $17.50 CAN
Publication date: July 1997

NOR THE BATTLE TO THE STRONG

Carl Jackson

From Imfe who is taken in slavery from Africa, Zero who is born a slave, Bam who lives to see emancipation, Tom who endures the long slow years of colonialism and Rocky who is active in the popular uprisings of the 1930s, *Nor the Battle to the Strong* is an unrivalled portrayal of the lives of five generations of an African Barbadian family. The careful research behind the novel gives the narrative rich and convincing texture, but it is the imaginative salvaging of the inner lives of this family which connects them to the present. Whilst frequently painful and disturbing, this is no recycled novel of abolitionist grievance, but an artistically shaped work of grief and hope. Jackson points to a longer historical context and a wider human truth in his reference to Ecclesiastes: 'The race is not to the swift, nor the battle to the strong, ... for time and chance happeneth to them all...'

This novel is part of an important return to historical subjects made by such contemporary Caribbean novelists as Caryl Phillips, David Dabydeen, Beryl Gilroy & Kevyn Arthur, and is an essential rewriting of the slavery narratives of earlier writers such as Edgar Mittelholzer. Whereas the latter co-opted the inhumanities of slavery to a pornography of violence, and restricted slave lives to the margins of his concerns, Jackson's treatment of the cruelties of the past is unflinching but controlled, and set within a larger context where the possibilities of redemption are never ruled out. Above all, he puts the historically voiceless at the articulate heart of his narrative.

Carl Jackson is the author of *East Wind in Paradise*, a political thriller published by New Beacon.

ISBN: 0-948833-97-1
Pages: 352pp
Price: £7.99 $14.00 US $17.50 CAN
Publication date: July 1997

INKLE AND YARICO

Beryl Gilroy

As a young man, Thomas Inkle sets out for Barbados to inspect the family sugar estates. On the way he is shipwrecked on a small West Indian island inhabited by Carib Indians. He alone escapes as his shipmates are slaughtered, and is rescued by Yarico, a Carib woman who takes him as, "an ideal, strange and obliging lover." So begins an encounter which has a profound effect on both.

Amongst the Caribs, Inkle is a mere child, whose survival depends entirely on Yarico's protection. But when he is rescued and taken with Yarico to the slave island of Barbados, she is entirely at his mercy.

Inkle and Yarico is loosely based on a "true" story, popular in the 17th and 18th centuries. Beryl Gilroy reinterprets its mythic dimensions from both a woman's and a black perspective, but above all she engages the reader in the psychological truths of her characters' experiences.

As an old man, Inkle recalls the Carib's stories as being like "fresh dreams, newly washed, newly woven and true to the daily lives of the community". *Inkle and Yarico* has the same magic and pertinence.

Beryl Gilroy is the author of *Frangipani House, Boy Sandwich, Sunlight on Sweet Water, Gather the Faces* and *In Praise of Love and Children.* The last three titles are published by Peepal Tree Press.

ISBN: 0-948833-98-X
Pages: 160
Price: £6.95
Publication date: July 1996

REQUIEM

Kwame Dawes

In these "shrines of remembrance" for the millions of the victims of transatlantic slavery, Kwame Dawes constructs a sequence which laments, rages, mourns, but also celebrates survival.

Inspired by the award-winning book, The Middle Passage: White Ships/Black Cargo, by the African-American artist Tom Feeling, these poems focus on individual moments in this holocaust which lasted nearly four hundred years. They both cauterize a lingering infection and offer the oil of healing.

In these taut lyric pieces, Dawes achieves what might seem impossible: saying something fresh about a subject which, despite attempts at historical amnesia, will not go away. He does it by eschewing sentimentality, rant or playing to the audience, black or white. His poems go to the heart of the historical experience and its contemporary reverberations.

Kwame Dawes won the prestigious Forward Poetry Prize in 1994 for his first collection, *Progeny of Air*. His second collection from Peepal Tree, *Prophets*, received wide critical acclaim.

> **Young, highly original and intelligent, unshakeable and unstoppable... he writes poetry as poetry should be written... the result is magic.**
>
> ***Lines Review***

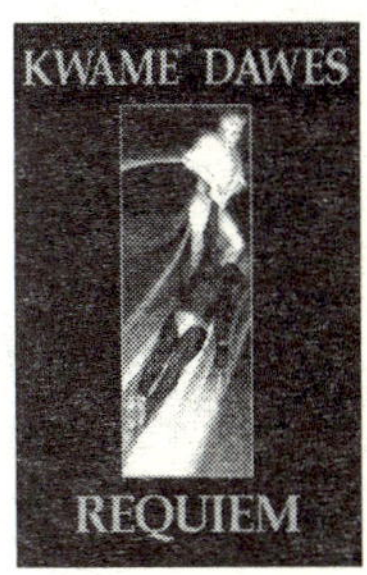

ISBN: 1-900715-07-4
Pages: 56
Price: £4.99
Publication date: November 1996

DISCUSSING COLUMBUS

Cyril Dabydeen

'Cyril Dabydeen is one of the most confident and accomplished voices in the Caribbean diaspora this side of the 20th century.'

Kamau Brathwaite

For Cyril Dabydeen, the historical figure of Columbus is an 'illustration of an odd and idiosyncratic destiny at work'. In this collection of poems, Dabydeen explores the personal confluences and ironies of a history which brought his ancestors as labourers from India to the Caribbean in an ironic inversion of Columbus' original mistake. On 'a deserted but peopled land' Dabydeen explores experiences of Canada and the Caribbean which simultaneously speak of a past of brutal genocide and tyranny and a present world of recreating newness, constantly awaiting rediscovery, constantly evolving from the heterogeneous convergencies which that voyage of 1492 began.

A long poem for voices, 'The Caribbees', concludes the collection, a reconstruction of the Amerindian/Columbian encounter told through a radical reworking of the Crusoe myth.

Cyril Dabydeen grew up in Guyana on the Rose Hall sugar estate. He worked as a teacher in Guyana before moving to Canada in 1970, where he has worked as a tree planter and more recently as a lecturer at the University of Ottawa. He is the author of, amongst other titles, *The Wizard Swami*, *Dark Swirl* and *Berbice Crossing* (fiction) and *Islands Lovelier than a Vision* (poetry), all published by Peepal Tree.

ISBN: 0-948833-57-2
Pages: 96pp
Price: £6.95 $12.00 US $15.00 CAN
Publication date: February 1997

COMING HOME & OTHER STORIES

June Henfrey

In the fields of whispering sugar cane, the rugged Atlantic coast of crashing breakers and the womb-like gullies of Barbados, the characters in these stories find a landscape which mirrors their inner lives. Set at crucial points in Caribbean history, from slavery to the present; from Nanny, who cannot bear another day's captivity when rumours of slavery's abolition reach the island, to Hilda, returning home after many years in Britain, these are strong and moving portrayals of women attempting to define themselves in situations where power is determined by race and gender.

Nanny knows that 'neither she nor others could reallycall their lives their own', but it is not only under slavery that June Henfrey's women confront this fact. In doing so, their lives enlarge our sense of history.

June Henfrey was born in Barbados in 1939. These stories were written during the two years before she died in 1992.

ISBN: 1-948833-67-X

Pages: 103pp

Price: £5.95 $10.50 US $13.00 CAN

Publication date: September 1994

SINGERMAN

Hazel D. Campbell

Realistic and magical, sombre and deeply comic, heroic and full of ironies, these stories explore the complexities of Caribbean reality through a variety of voices and forms.

In 'Jacob Bubbles', a short novella, Campbell connects the contemporary Jamaica of polical gang warfare to the past of slavery through the characters of Joseph, a runaway slave and his descendant, Jacob Bubbles, the fearsome leader of the Suckdust Posse. When Jacob Bubbles meets his death at the hands of Pantyhose, the female leader of a rival gang, a memory path opens in his head:

'to Papa Tee, a regular bullbucker and duppy conqueror chopping at human flesh; swearing at mothers with babies he had no intention of supporting; swearing in frustration in the line at the docks – no work this week, again! The blood leaking from him belonged to all of them – to Johnson, Papa Tee's father working the piece of land on the hillside which barely gave him enough to eat; to Cris-Cris, digging earth and coughing blood in a strange Spanish-speaking country; to Maas Sam, the obeah man at whom ghosts laughed; to William, chased off the estate because he asked for more wages; to all of them passing swiftly back into time; back to Jacob, the runaway slave pausing under a tree to rearrange his human burdens so that he could make a faster escape into the forest, up into the mountains to freedom.'

In these stories there is an acute perception of the ways in which poverty, racism and sexism can maim the spirit. But if there is one overarching vision, it is of the redemptive power of hope and love and the people's capacity to rise out of enslavements old and new.

ISBN: 0-948833-44-0
Pages: 155pp
Price: £4.95 $9.50 US $11.00 CAN
Publication date: 1991